Developing Nations

Berna Miller and James D. Torr, *Book Editors*

Daniel Leone, *President*
Bonnie Szumski, *Publisher*
Scott Barbour, *Managing Editor*
Helen Cothran, *Senior Editor*

CURRENT CONTROVERSIES

GREENHAVEN
PRESS®

THOMSON
™
GALE

San Diego • Detroit • New York • San Francisco • Cleveland
New Haven, Conn. • Waterville, Maine • London • Munich

LIBRARY OF CONGRESS CATALOGING-IN-PUBLICATION DATA

Developing nations / Berna Miller, James D. Torr, book editors.
    p. cm. — (Current controversies)
Includes bibliographical references and index.
ISBN 0-7377-1179-5 (pbk. : alk. paper) — ISBN 0-7377-1180-9 (lib. : alk. paper)
    1. Developing countries—Economic conditions—21st century. 2. Developing countries—Social conditions—21st century. 3. Globalization—Economic aspect—Developing countries. 4. Globalization—Social aspect—Developing countries. 5. Globalization—Moral and ethical aspect—Developing countries. I. Miller, Berna. II. Torr, James D., 1974– . III. Series.
HC59.7 .D427 2003
330.9172'4—dc21
                                                                                          2002033081

Printed in the United States of America

Contents

Regulations against air pollution in the developing world have traditionally been lax or nonexistent. As a result, air pollution kills about 750,000 people annually in developing countries.

Chapter 2: Will Globalization Harm Developing Nations?

Yes: Globalization Will Harm Developing Nations

No: Globalization Will Benefit Developing Nations

Chapter 3: Should Industrialized Nations Play an Active Role in the Developing World?

Chapter 4: Can Democracy Succeed in Developing Nations?

Since the 1980s, worldwide efforts to promote democracy have given rise
to a "democracy industry"—a huge international network of government
and nonprofit organizations that work to aid developing nations in implementing free elections and other democratic institutions. But too often,
this democracy industry is willing to put a "stamp of approval" on elections and newly instituted regimes that are anything but democratic.

pared to 77 in the United States. On average, Angolan women bear almost seven children each, compared with two in the United States. According to a United Nations International Children's Fund (UNICEF) report, "the condition of children in Angola remains catastrophic. The under-five mortality rate is the second highest in the world, with one child dying every three minutes, or 420 children dying every day."

Angola has little in the way of the transportation or technology infrastructure Americans take for granted. Three-fourths of its roads are unpaved, and much of the railroad system is unusable due to land mines used during the civil war. Most citizens have little access to basic technology. While many American homes have multiple phones, televisions, and radios, there are a total of about 62,000 regular telephones, 7,000 cell phones, 630,000 radios, and 150,000 televisions for 10 million Angolan citizens. The first automatic-teller machine for a bank is expected by the end of 2002.

Angola's level of economic, social, and industrial achievement may now undergo significant change. On April 3, 2002, Angola reached a peace agreement that ended its civil war. The country now faces the dual challenge of recovering from decades of war while at the same time trying to achieve economic and social development.

Development for Angola, as for other nations, clearly entails raising the standard of living of its citizens. According to Michael Todaro, development involves expanding choices, but also more concrete actions by governments to improve the quality of human lives by "provision of basic needs, reducing inequality, raising living standards through appropriate economic growth . . . and expanding freedom of choice in the market and beyond." Indeed, many of the world's leaders believe that development involves not just economic growth, but also something more. In the words of Pope Paul VI, "to speak of development, is in effect to show as much concern for social progress as for economic growth." To that end, the United Nations defines development as "the process of enlarging people's choices . . . to lead a long and healthy life, to acquire knowledge and to have access to the resources needed for a decent standard of living."

What problems developing nations have, what exactly development entails, and the best way to achieve development is highly contested. The authors in *Current Controversies: Developing Nations* provide insight on the different problems facing developing nations, as well as possible solutions, in the following chapters: What Are the Problems Facing Developing Nations? Does Globalization Harm Developing Nations? Should Industrialized Nations Play an Active Role in the Developing World? Can Democracy Succeed in Developing Nations? Roughly 60 percent of the world's people (excluding China) live in developing nations; the essays in this volume are intended to give readers a better understanding of the challenges these people face.

Chapter 1

What Are the Problems Facing Developing Nations?

groups, or the socially disadvantaged. That is why facilitating the empowerment of poor people—by making state and social institutions more responsive to them—is also key to reducing poverty.

Vulnerability to external and largely uncontrollable events—illness, violence, economic shocks, bad weather, natural disasters—reinforces poor people's sense of ill-being, exacerbates their material poverty, and weakens their bargaining position. That is why enhancing security—by reducing the risk of such events as wars, disease, economic crises, and natural disasters—is key to reducing poverty. And so is reducing poor people's vulnerability to risks and putting in place mechanisms to help them cope with adverse shocks.

Poverty in an Unequal World

The world has deep poverty amid plenty. Of the world's 6 billion people 2.8 billion—almost half—live on less than $2 a day, and 1.2 billion—a fifth—live on less than $1 a day, with 44 percent living in South Asia (figure 1). In rich countries fewer than 1 child in 100 does not reach its fifth birthday, while in the poorest countries as many as a fifth of children do not. And while in rich countries fewer than 5 percent of all children under five are malnourished, in poor countries as many as 50 percent are.

Figure 1. Where the Developing World's Poor Live

Distribution of population living on less than $1 a day, 1998 (1.2 billion)

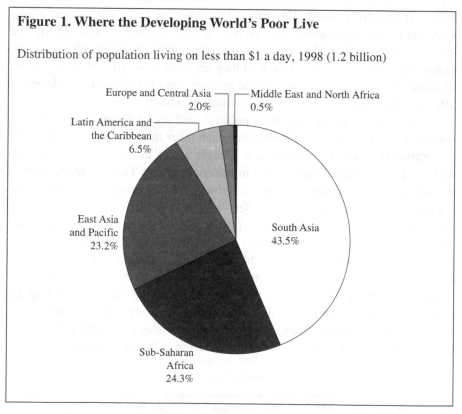

Europe and Central Asia — 2.0%
Middle East and North Africa — 0.5%
Latin America and the Caribbean — 6.5%
East Asia and Pacific — 23.2%
South Asia — 43.5%
Sub-Saharan Africa — 24.3%

This destitution persists even though human conditions have improved more in the past century than in the rest of history—global wealth, global connections, and technological capabilities have never been greater. But the distribution of these global gains is extraordinarily unequal. The average income in the richest 20 countries is 37 times the average in the poorest 20—a gap that has doubled in the past 40 years. And the experience in different parts of the world has been very diverse. In East Asia the number of people living on less than $1 a day fell from around 420 million to around 280 million between 1987 and 1998—even after the setbacks of the financial crisis. Yet in Latin America, South Asia, and Sub-Saharan Africa the numbers of poor people have been rising. And in the countries of Europe and Central Asia in transition to market economies, the number of people living on less than $1 a day rose more than twentyfold.

There have also been major advances and serious setbacks in crucial nonincome measures of poverty. India has seen marked progress in girls attending school, and in the most advanced state, Kerala, life expectancy is greater than in other places with many times the level of income (such as Washington, D.C.). Yet in countries at the center of the HIV/AIDS epidemic in Africa, such as Botswana and Zimbabwe, one in four adults is infected, AIDS orphans are becoming an overwhelming burden on both traditional and formal support mechanisms, and all the gains in life expectancy since the middle of the 20th century will soon be wiped out. The varying infant mortality rates across the world Sub-Saharan Africa's is 15 times that of high-income countries—give an idea of this widely differing experience.

> *"Of the world's 6 billion people 2.8 billion—almost half—live on less than $2 a day."*

Experiences are also vastly different at subnational levels and for ethnic minorities and women. Different regions in countries benefit to very different extents from growth. In Mexico, for example, total poverty fell—though modestly—in the early 1990s, but rose in the poorer Southeast. Inequalities also exist across different ethnic groups in many countries. In some African countries infant mortality rates are lower among politically powerful ethnic groups, and in Latin American countries indigenous groups often have less than three-quarters the schooling on average of nonindigenous groups. And women continue to be more disadvantaged than men. In South Asia women have only about half as many years of education as men, and female enrollment rates at the secondary level are only two-thirds the male rates.

Faced with this picture of global poverty and inequality, the international community has set itself several goals for the opening years of the century, based on discussions at various United Nations conferences in the 1990s. These international development goals, most for 2015, include reducing income poverty and human deprivation in many dimensions (the benchmarks are figures for 1990):

- Reduce by half the proportion of people living in extreme income poverty (living on less than $1 a day).
- Ensure universal primary education.
- Eliminate gender disparity in primary and secondary education (by 2005).
- Reduce infant and child mortality by two-thirds.
- Reduce maternal mortality by three-quarters.
- Ensure universal access to reproductive health services.
- Implement national strategies for sustainable development in every country by 2005, so as to reverse the loss of environmental resources by 2015.

These will have to be achieved in a world whose population will grow by some 2 billion in the next 25 years, with 97 percent of that increase in developing countries. Studies of what must be done to achieve these goals reveal the magnitude of the challenge. For example, cutting income poverty by half between 1990 and 2015 would require a compound rate of decline of 2.7 percent a year over those 25 years. The World Bank's latest estimates indicate a reduction of approximately 1.7 percent a year between 1990 and 1998. Much of the slow progress observed in some regions is due to low or negative growth. In some cases rising inequality compounded this effect; this was particularly so in some countries in the former Soviet Union. The current pace of educational enrollment is unlikely to bring universal primary education, especially in Sub-Saharan Africa. Reducing infant mortality rates by two-thirds between 1990 and 2015 would have required a 30 percent decline between 1990 and 1998, far greater than the 10 percent developing countries experienced. In some parts of Sub-Saharan Africa infant mortality is actually on the rise, partly as a result of the AIDS epidemic. And maternal mortality ratios are declining too slowly to meet the goals.

Attaining the international development goals will require actions to spur economic growth and reduce income inequality, but even equitable growth will not be enough to achieve the goals for health and education. Reducing infant and child mortality rates by two-thirds depends on halting the spread of HIV/AIDS, increasing the capacity of developing countries' health systems to deliver more health services, and ensuring that technological progress in the medical field spills

> *"In the 1970s awareness grew that physical capital was not enough [to reduce global poverty], and that at least as important were health and education."*

over to benefit the developing world. And meeting the gender equality goals in education will require specific policy measures to address the cultural, social, and economic barriers that prevent girls from attending school. Furthermore, actions to ensure greater environmental sustainability will be crucial in augmenting the assets available to poor people and in reducing the long-term incidence of poverty. These actions will all interact to push toward the achievement of the goals. Hence the need for a broader, more comprehensive strategy to fight poverty.

A Strategy for Poverty Reduction

The approach to reducing poverty has evolved over the past 50 years in response to deepening understanding of the complexity of development. In the 1950s and 1960s many viewed large investments in physical capital and infrastructure as the primary means of development.

In the 1970s awareness grew that physical capital was not enough, and that at least as important were health and education. *World Development Report 1980* articulated this understanding and argued that improvements in health and education were important not only in their own right but also to promote growth in the incomes of poor people.

The 1980s saw another shift of emphasis following the debt crisis and global recession and the contrasting experiences of East Asia and Latin America, South Asia, and Sub-Saharan Africa. Emphasis was placed on improving economic management and allowing greater play for market forces. *World Development Report 1990: Poverty* proposed a two-part strategy: promoting labor-intensive growth through economic openness and investment in infrastructure and providing basic services to poor people in health and education.

In the 1990s governance and institutions moved toward center stage—as did issues of vulnerability at the local and national levels. This report builds on the earlier strategies in the light of the cumulative evidence and experience of the past decade—and in the light of the changed global context. It proposes a strategy for attacking poverty in three ways: promoting opportunity, facilitating empowerment, and enhancing security.

• *Promoting opportunity.* Poor people consistently emphasize the centrality of material opportunities. This means jobs, credit, roads, electricity, markets for their produce, and the schools, water, sanitation, and health services that underpin the health and skills essential for work. Overall economic growth is crucial for generating opportunity. So is the pattern or quality of growth. Market reforms can be central in expanding opportunities for poor people, but reforms need to reflect local institutional and structural conditions. And mechanisms need to be in place to create new opportunities and compensate the potential losers in transitions. In societies with high inequality, greater equity is particularly important for rapid progress in reducing poverty. This requires action by the state to support the buildup of human, land, and infrastructure assets that poor people own or to which they have access.

• *Facilitating empowerment.* The choice and implementation of public actions that are responsive to the needs of poor people depend on the interaction of political, social, and other institutional processes. Access to market opportunities and to public sector services is often strongly influenced by state and social institutions, which must be responsive and accountable to poor people. Achieving access, responsibility, and accountability is intrinsically political and requires active collaboration among poor people, the middle class, and other groups in society. Active collaboration can be greatly facilitated by changes in governance that make public administration, legal institutions, and public service delivery more efficient and accountable to all citizens—and by strengthening the participation of poor people in political processes and local decisionmaking. Also important is removing the social and institutional barriers that result from distinctions of gender, ethnicity, and social status. Sound and responsive institutions are not only important to benefit the poor but are also fundamental to the overall growth process.

> *"Poverty is more than inadequate income or human development—it is also vulnerability and a lack of voice, power, and representation."*

• *Enhancing security.* Reducing vulnerability—to economic shocks, natural disasters, ill health, disability, and personal violence—is an intrinsic part of enhancing well-being and encourages investment in human capital and in higher-risk, higher-return activities. This requires effective national action to manage the risk of economywide shocks and effective mechanisms to reduce the risks faced by poor people, including health- and weather-related risks. It also requires building the assets of poor people, diversifying household activities, and providing a range of insurance mechanisms to cope with adverse shocks—from public work to stay-in-school programs and health insurance.

There is no hierarchy of importance. The elements are deeply complementary. Each part of the strategy affects underlying causes of poverty addressed by the other two. For example, promoting opportunity through assets and market access increases the independence of poor people and thus empowers them by strengthening their bargaining position relative to state and society. It also enhances security, since an adequate stock of assets is a buffer against adverse shocks. Similarly, strengthening democratic institutions and empowering women and disadvantaged ethnic and racial groups—say, by eliminating legal discrimination against them—expand the economic opportunities for the poor and socially excluded. Strengthening organizations of poor people can help to ensure service delivery and policy choices responsive to the needs of poor people and can reduce corruption and arbitrariness in state actions as well. And if poor people do more in monitoring and controlling the local delivery of social services, public spending is more likely to help them during crises. Finally, helping poor people cope with shocks and manage risks puts them in a better position to take advantage of emerging market opportunities. That is why this [viewpoint] advocates a comprehensive approach to attacking poverty. . . .

[This] strategy . . . recognizes that poverty is more than inadequate income or human development—it is also vulnerability and a lack of voice, power, and representation. With this multidimensional view of poverty comes greater complexity in poverty reduction strategies, because more factors—such as social and cultural forces—need to be taken into account.

The way to deal with this complexity is through empowerment and participation—local, national, and international. National governments should be fully accountable to their citizenry for the development path they pursue. Participatory mechanisms can provide voice to women and men, especially those from poor and excluded segments of society. The design of decentralized agencies and services needs to reflect local conditions, social structures, and cultural norms and heritage. And international institutions should listen to—and promote—the interests of poor people. The poor are the main actors in the fight against poverty. And they must be brought center stage in designing, implementing, and monitoring antipoverty strategies.

There is an important role in this for rich countries and international organizations. If a developing country has a coherent and effective homegrown program of poverty reduction, it should receive strong support—to bring health and education to its people, to remove want and vulnerability. At the same time global forces need to be harnessed for poor people and poor countries, so that they are not left behind by scientific and medical advances. Promoting global financial and environmental stability—and lowering market barriers to the products and services of poor countries—should be a core part of the strategy.

A divergent world? Or an inclusive one? A world with poverty? Or a world free of poverty? Simultaneous actions to expand opportunity, empowerment, and security can create a new dynamic for change that will make it possible to tackle human deprivation and create just societies that are also competitive and productive. If the developing world and the international community work together to combine this insight with real resources, both financial and those embodied in people and institutions—their experience, knowledge, and imagination—the 21st century will see rapid progress in the fight to end poverty.

Hunger Is a Serious Problem in Developing Nations

by George McGovern

About the author: *George McGovern was a U.S. senator from 1963 to 1984 and the Democratic candidate for president in 1972. This viewpoint is based on excerpts from his book* The Third Freedom: Ending Hunger in Our Time.

It is impossible to evaluate with dollars the real cost of hunger. What is the value of a human life? The twentieth century was the most violent in human history, with nearly 150 million people killed by war. But in just the last half of that century nearly three times as many died of malnutrition or related causes. How does one put a dollar figure on this terrible toll silently collected by the Grim Reaper? What is the cost of 800 million hungry people dragging through shortened and miserable lives, unable to study, work, play or otherwise function normally because of the ever-present drain of hunger and malnutrition on body, mind and spirit? What is the cost of millions of young mothers breaking under the despair of watching their children waste away and die from malnutrition? This is a problem we can resolve at a fraction of the cost of ignoring it.

Encouraging Statistics

Hunger is a political condition. The earth has enough knowledge and re-sources to eradicate this ancient scourge. Hunger has plagued the world for thousands of years. But ending it is a greater moral imperative now than ever before, because for the first time humanity has the instruments in hand to defeat this cruel enemy at a very reasonable cost. We have the ability to provide food for all within the next three decades. Consider just one encouraging statistic: When I ran for the presidency in 1972, 35 per cent of the world's people were hungry. By 1996, while the global population had expanded, only 17 per cent of the earth's people were hungry—half the percentage of three decades ago. This is an impressive fact, particularly in view of the gloomy prophecies of the

1960s that population growth was racing ahead of food production. Widespread famines across the Third World were also predicted. Clearly the gains in food production from scientific farming, including the Green Revolution, plus the slowing of population growth, have reduced hunger in the developing countries.

Here are some other encouraging statistics: the world now produces a quantity of grain that, if distributed evenly, would provide everyone with 3,500 calories per day, more than enough for an optimal diet. This does not even count vegetables, fruits, fish, meat, poultry, edible oils, nuts, root crops, or dairy products. Despite the dire predictions that the world's population would soon outstrip food production, it has been the other way

> *"Hunger is a political condition. The earth has enough knowledge and resources to eradicate this ancient scourge."*

around: food production has risen a full 16 per cent above population growth. The American Association for the Advancement of Science has noted that 78 per cent of the world's malnourished children live in countries with food surpluses. Clearly, this condition indicates a need for a keener social conscience and better political leadership. A 1996 United Nations survey that is regarded as the most accurate forecast available estimated that world population will peak and then level off near the year 2050 at just under 10 billion—an increase of 4 billion over the present total. Population may then decline somewhat, because of lower birth rates. Such predictions are uncertain. It may be that advances in medicine and health care will enable people to live longer, thus offsetting declining birth rates. Although a population of 10 billion will tax some resources, projected increases in food production indicate that the world can feed that many people a half-century from now. As we will see from the pages that follow, the nations and peoples of the world will have to take a series of commonsense steps to ensure that everyone is fed. But there is no need for panic or scare tactics. There is enough food to go around now and for at least the next half-century. The world is not going to run out of food for all. Those readers young enough to be around in the year 2050 will need to consider other measures that will take the world safely through the last half of the century, to 2100. But who can even guess what scientific gains will come into the hands and minds of future generations?

Having grappled for years with the global hunger challenge and the American domestic condition, I am sure that we have the resources and the knowledge to end hunger everywhere. The big question is: Do we have the political leadership and the will to end this scourge in our time?

The Cost of Hunger

One of my admired friends of long standing was the late Archbishop Dom Helder Camara of Brazil. He once observed: "When I give food to the poor, they call me a saint. When I ask why the poor have no food, they call me a communist." I learned much about the burdens and hurts of the poor from this good man.

Two questions need to be considered together in a treatise about world hunger: (1) What would it cost for the nations of the world, acting through the United Nations, to end hunger? and (2) What will be the cost if we permit hunger to continue at its present level? Of the scores of experts with the UN agencies in Rome chiefly involved in the global hunger issue, I have yet to meet a single one—conservative, liberal or mugwump—who does not believe that the cost to the world of hunger is vastly greater than the cost of ending it. I can think of no investment that would profit the international community more than erasing hunger from the face of the earth.

So what will it cost? Beyond what the United States and other countries are now doing, it will take an estimated $5 billion a year, of which $1.2 billion would come from the United States. If this annual allocation were continued for fifteen years, until 2015, we could reduce the 800 million hungry people by half. To erase hunger for the remaining 400 million would cost about the same if it were to be accomplished in the fifteen years leading up to the year 2030.

The United States Agency for International Development puts the cost at $2.6 billion annually, whereas the UN Food and Agriculture Organization estimates the cost higher at $6 billion. My figure of $5 billion annually—which is based on my own judgement of the cost of some of the

> *"I can think of no investment that would profit the international community more than erasing hunger from the face of the earth."*

steps I would like to see taken, including especially a universal school lunch programme for every child in the world—is $2.4 billion higher than USAID's but still a billion below the United Nations figure. I concur with the estimate of the respected Bread for the World Institute in Silver Spring, Maryland, that it would take another $5 billion—largely in updating our food stamp programme—to meet the needs of the 31 million inadequately fed Americans. Thus, the total American cost internationally and domestically would be an additional $6.2 billion a year—a fraction of what we now spend on cigarettes, beer or cosmetics. If we decided to enact a modest increase in the minimum wage, we could cut the increase in food stamps in half.

What will it cost if we don't end the hunger that now afflicts so many of our fellow humans? The World Bank has concluded that each year malnutrition causes the loss of 46 million years of productive life, at a cost of $16 billion annually, several times the cost of ending hunger and turning this loss into productive gain.

But victory over hunger will not come without the assistance of those countries able to help, including the European nations, Japan, Canada, Australia, Argentina and the OPEC oil States. And before the battle is over, perhaps it can be joined by China, India and Russia. Of equal or greater importance is the need for reform in the developing countries if hunger is to be ended. This means improved farming methods; the conservation and wiser use of the earth's limited water resources; more rights and opportunities, especially education, for the girls and women of the Third World; a greater measure of democratic government responsive to basic human needs, including food security; and a substitution of common-sense negotiation of differences instead of the murderous civil, ethnic and nationalistic conflicts that have torn up people, property and land across the Third World. It is estimated that 10 per cent of the world's hungry people are in that condition because of the disruptions of war and other civil strife. People in villages and on farms, including poor women and men, as well as city dwellers, need to be involved in political and economic decisions that affect their lives. Education and democracy may be the most powerful combatants in the war on hunger and poverty. These are a few of the conditions that need to be confronted to build for the first time the architecture of food security on our planet.

A Worldwide School Lunch Programme

Of the world's hungry people, 300 million are school-age children. Not only do they bear the pangs of hunger but also their malnutrition leads to loss of energy, listlessness and vulnerability to diseases of all kinds. Hungry children cannot function well in school—if, indeed, they are able to attend school at all. Hunger and malnutrition in childhood years can stunt the body and mind for a lifetime. Every minute, more than ten children under the age of five die of hunger. No one can even guess at the vastly larger number of older children and adults who lead damaged lives because of malnutrition in their fetal or infant days.

A nutritious, balanced school lunch for every child is the best investment we can make in the health, education and global society of the future. After President John Kennedy appointed me in 1961 to head the United States Food for Peace Program, I was contacted by a remarkable Catholic priest who was stationed with the Maryknoll Fathers in the impoverished Puno area of Peru. Father Dan McClellan convinced me that if the United States could supply the food, the Maryknoll Fathers could administer a school lunch programme in the Puno region.

"Of the world's hungry people, 300 million are school-age children."

On 12 May 1961, Prime Minister Pedro Beltran of Peru came to my office at the White House to place his signature on an agreement for school lunches for 30,000 Puno students, to be administered by the Maryknoll Fathers. At the Prime Minister's suggestion, however, the food was given to the children as a breakfast upon their arrival at school. Mr. Beltran told us that the children did not receive enough food at home to begin the day. A school breakfast would be an incentive for students to be on time and would give them enough energy for the day's educational activities. Perhaps a glass of milk with a cookie or a piece of bread could be added at midday as an energy pickup.

In the Puno area, illiteracy was 90 per cent. Only a meagre fraction of the students were in school. In some schools, nine out of ten students dropped out before completing the sixth grade. Schoolchildren were seriously handicapped by the lethargy and drowsiness that resulted from malnutrition. But within six months after the United States–assisted school lunch programme began in the fall of 1961, teachers noted that attendance had nearly doubled and academic performance had improved dramatically.

> *"If education is the key to development in the Third World, the school lunch is the key to unlocking the education door."*

The signing by Prime Minister Beltran and me signalled a new emphasis in Food for Peace on United States–assisted school feeding programmes. This was the first United States agreement of its kind. By 1964, 12 million, or one out of three, schoolchildren in South America were being fed a nutritious daily lunch through Food for Peace.

In Asia, Africa and Latin America, wherever we have experimented with school lunches, we have seen school attendance double in a year or so; grades have also climbed. A daily lunch is the surest magnet for drawing children to school that anyone has yet devised. This is a very important fact because of the world's 300 million school-age children, 130 million are illiterate and not attending school. If education is the key to development in the Third World, the school lunch is the key to unlocking the education door. Of the 130 million not attending school most are girls because of favouritism toward boys. These illiterate girls marry at the age of eleven, twelve or thirteen, and have an average of six children. Girls who go to school marry later and have an average of 2.9 children. A good school lunch is the best way yet found to get both girls and boys into school. The lowly school lunch indirectly produces healthier youngsters, advances education, reduces the birth rate and provides a profitable market for the surplus farm commodities of the United States and other surplus-producing countries.

Implementing the Programme

A school lunch every day for every child in the world would require the labour and initiative of many people and nations. In the United States, we would need to call on churches, synagogues and mosques, as well as our secular philanthropic groups. Such religious and charitable institutions are already engaged in administering and distributing food relief abroad. But they should be urged and enabled to do much more. Wherever such private agencies can take the place of Government in administering and monitoring school lunches or other food programmes, they should be encouraged to do so. Also, wherever possible, local farmers should be given an opportunity to supply food at a fair price to the local school lunch programme. When locally produced food is available, food aid can be acquired more cheaply from recipient or neighbouring countries than from more distant sources where shipping and handling charges would be significant. The programme would still require substantial dairy, livestock and cereal grain production from the United States and other surplus-producing countries, because local supplies are not always equal to the demand. Beyond this, private foundations, labour unions, corporations and individuals should consider contributing to this cause. Such contributions should go to the UN World Food Programme in Rome.

I would estimate the start-up costs covering the first two years of a school lunch programme seriously intended to be universal at $3 billion. With the United States initially in the lead, our portion might reach half of that figure— $1.5 billion spread out over two years. The bulk of that would be in surplus commodities purchased in the American market. As more and more students enrolled in the programme, costs would increase, but we may hope that more and more countries would join in helping to finance the programme, so American costs would probably not increase significantly, if at all. Also, expected contributions from private foundations, corporations, labour unions and individuals should hold down government costs.

It is my hope that the receiving Governments would themselves be able to take over and finance the programme within five or six years. Meanwhile, it would be under the instructional and monitoring eyes of the World Food Programme, which has highly capable and experienced people in field offices within eighty countries.

Obesity Is a Growing Problem in Developing Nations

by Ellen Ruppel Shell

About the author: *Ellen Ruppel Shell is a correspondent for the* Atlantic Monthly *and codirector of the Knight Center for Science and Medical Journalism at Boston University.*

In Kosrae, an island in Micronesia, new arrivals are a curiosity, and it seemed that half the island had come to greet me and Steven Auerbacb, a Manhattan-based medical epidemiologist and an officer in the U.S. Public Health Service who had worked in Micronesia in the early 1990s, when we visited last year. Dazed from our 8,000-mile journey, we groped our way down the pockmarked coastal road, driving past groves of trees bent nearly double under loads of bananas, papayas, and breadfruit. We were on our way to a funeral feast.

We arrived to find the feast in full swing. Young men in lawn chairs played cards, while toddlers squatted, transfixed, around a television screen blaring taped cartoons. Hovering women filled plates and wiped faces. Perhaps a hundred people were there, and the dead man's wife looked bored. The deceased, buried four weeks earlier in a nearby crypt, seemed almost beside the point.

New World Syndrome

Kosraeans die young (the man in the crypt was fifty-six), but not for reasons commonly associated with the developing world. There is no famine here, and with the notable exception of upper-respiratory infections, little evidence of the diseases that cut life short in, for example, sub-Saharan Africa. The big killer in Kosrae—what some epidemiologists call New World syndrome—is a constellation of maladies brought on not by microbes or parasites but by the assault of rapid Westernization on traditional cultures. Diabetes, heart disease, and high blood pressure—scourges of affluence that long ago eclipsed infectious diseases as killers in the West—have only recently appeared here.

We sat with the dead man's brother-in-law, who told us that he expects to die soon too. His sister's husband died of heart disease; he himself will likely die of diabetes. "But I am fifty-seven, an old man, so this is of no matter," he said. He worried more about the young people. Nodding toward the cardplayers nearby, he said that it was not uncommon for them to gather to mourn a man or woman of thirty.

Kosrae was at one time a mighty kingdom, with Lelu its capital. Today Lelu is still the state's largest and most densely populated village, a jumble of tin-roofed huts connected to Kosrae proper by a causeway. We went to Lelu to see the ruins of the ancient city, built 600 years ago of immense basalt "logs." Exhausted by the heat, we ducked into a nearby general store to get a cold drink. Inside we found row after row of canned goods: Spam and corned beef and Vienna sausages in fancy tins. There were cake and muffin mixes from the United States, ramen-noodle soup from the Philippines, flats of soda and Budweiser beer, shelves of candy bars and potato chips. An entire freezer was reserved for turkey tails—a fatty, gristly hunk of the bird which is generally regarded as inedible in the United States. The freezer was empty. Turkey tails are so popular, we were told, that the month's shipment was long gone.

In the handful of other grocery stores scattered around the island we found plenty of salty, sweet, and fatty imports—but no fresh bananas, papayas, breadfruit, coconut, or mangoes. Apart from a fish shack or two and a few forlorn stands hawking bags of the island's famous—and costly—green tangerines, there was nowhere to buy local produce on the island. We were told that most Kosraeans once grew fruits and vegetables on family plots, and pulled tuna and reef fish from the sea. But the majority of modern Kosraeans don't have time or energy to farm or fish—they are too busy with their office jobs.

Kosrae is the smallest of four island states that make up the Federated States of Micronesia (FSM), the largest and most populous political entity to emerge from the Trust Territory of the Pacific Islands, which placed the islands under U.S. administration after World War II. In 1986 Micronesia implemented a Compact of Free Association with the United States, which dissolved its trust status. In order to sustain a security partnership, the United States is still the FSM's chief benefactor, supplying the bulk of its revenue—about $100 million—in aid each year. The bureaucracy required to manage and distribute this windfall continues to be Kosrae's single largest employer.

> *"New World syndrome . . . is a constellation of maladies brought on . . . by the assault of rapid Westernization on traditional cultures."*

Few if any of its jobs demand the skill or physical effort required by the traditional work of fishing and farming. Physical exertion has been further discouraged by expansion of the coastal road and the steady importation of cars, some bought with the help of government money. To walk in Kosrae is to announce that one is too poor to ride, and Kosraeans offer a lift to every casual stroller.

This newfound convenience comes at a high price, as a visit to Kosrae's state hospital revealed. A low-slung concrete structure with greasy windows and no air-conditioning, it is poorly equipped to handle anything but basic health needs. Patients with serious problems are airlifted to Guam or the Philippines. The hospital director, a former Vice President of Micronesia, confessed to us that he and his wife travel abroad for even routine checkups.

An Obesity Epidemic

The hospital's inpatient ward has perhaps two dozen beds, and nineteen were occupied on the morning we visited. Thirteen people were there for complications of diet-related diabetes and two for heart conditions. Paul Skilling, a Kosraean family doctor, lamented that cases of diabetes, hypertension, and heart disease are as common as coconuts on his island. Another doctor half joked that even health-care professionals are at risk. "Look at me" he said, pointing to his paunch. "I am myself obese. My body-mass index is thirty-two. How long before I have these diseases?"

The doctor was indeed obese, but his body-mass index was only slightly higher than average for a Kosraean adult. In 1993–1994 the Micronesian Department of Health, with funding from the U.S. Centers for Disease Control, screened almost all the adults on the island and found that nearly 85 percent of those aged forty-five to sixty-four were obese. Non-insulin-dependent diabetes mellitus, heart disease, and hypertension are closely linked to obesity, so it is perhaps not surprising that more than a quarter of Kosraeans in this age group were also diabetic, and more than a third suffered from high blood pressure. (Noninsulin-dependent diabetes mellitus, or NIDDM, the kind that afflicts Micronesia, is also known as Type II or adult-onset diabetes; "diabetes" here refers to this type.) Vita Skilling, the island's chief of preventive health services, told us that efforts to reverse this trend have been disappointing. "Here you buy imported food in the store to show that you have money," she said. "Even if you don't have much money, you can buy turkey tails."

> *"The [non-insulin-dependent diabetes mellitus] global epidemic is just the tip of a massive social problem now facing developing countries."*

In Kosrae 90 percent of adult surgical admissions are linked to diabetes, and of these many are for amputations necessitated by vascular breakdown. There are more cases of renal failure than the hospital can handle, and cardiovascular disease is pervasive. And in Kosrae ill health hits early—frequently men and women have a first heart attack in their late twenties.

New World syndrome has taken hold throughout much of the South Pacific. The problem in Kosrae pales by comparison with that in the Republic of Nauru, a tiny, crowded island known as the Kuwait of the South Pacific. Nauru's citizens grew rich from the mining of phosphate deposits, which long ago eclipsed fishing as the state's major revenue source and are now nearly depleted. This rocky island's few patches of arable land were laid waste years ago by mining, so Nauruans subsist almost entirely on imports. Prosperity has brought them Japanese televisions, German luxury sedans, and Australian filet mignon. It has also brought them what Auerbach calls "the worst of 1950s American cuisine"—processed foods with plenty of fat, salt, sugar,

> *"All measures indicate that the greatest impact of obesity-related disorders will continue to be in newly industrialized and developing nations."*

and refined starches. As a result Nauruans have among the highest rates of obesity and diabetes on the planet, and a life expectancy of only fifty-five. In contrast, the region's poorest nation—Kiribati, thirty-three islands that straddle the Equator, with little money for imported food or anything else—has in its rural regions the lowest rates of noncommunicable disease in the South Pacific. . . .

Paul Zimmet, an Australian physician and researcher who specializes in the study of noncommunicable diseases, wrote in 1996 that "the [non-insulin-dependent diabetes mellitus] global epidemic is just the tip of a massive social problem now facing developing countries." Zimmet implicated the "coca-colonization" that has devastated local customs and economies and led to ill health. Rates of obesity and diabetes have skyrocketed around the globe, but particularly among traditional peoples in transition—Polynesians, Native Americans, and aboriginal Australians; Asian Indian emigrants to Fiji, South Africa, and Britain; and Chinese emigrants to Singapore, Taiwan, and Hong Kong.

The "Thrifty Genotype"

Although the rapid introduction of processed foods and other conveniences is certainly the proximate force behind this trend, scientists are also looking at genetic components. Jeffrey Friedman, a professor and the head of the Laboratory of Molecular Genetics at the Howard Hughes Medical Institute at Rockefeller University, in New York, is investigating why some Kosraeans manage to escape the hazards of coca-colonization while others succumb. To Friedman and his team, the interesting question is not why so many sedentary, office-bound, Spam-loving Kosraeans are obese but why not all of them are.

Kosraeans, like all natives of Micronesia, trace their ancestry back 2,000 years to a handful of Indo-Malayan mariners. Driven by fear, religious persecution, greed, or foolhardiness, this small band settled the Pacific. Those who landed on Kosrae developed a feudal society that went largely unnoticed by the West until 1824, when a French research vessel, the *Coquille*, dropped anchor nearby. Rene Primevere Lesson, the ship's doctor, described Kosraeans as "advanced people of a high civilization, to judge from the vestiges of customs, tradition such as the authority of the chiefs, classes of society, and the remnants of the arts which they still practice." The women, he wrote, had "black eyes full of fire and a mouth full of superb teeth . . . but a tendency to become fat." He also observed that considering the island's bounty, its population of about 3,000 was surprisingly small. (Easter Island, in Polynesia, was then supporting a population of at least 7,000 with roughly the same land mass and a less hospitable climate.) Studies later supported local lore that a much larger population had been diminished by starvation after typhoons devastated the island's food supply. The population continued to dwindle throughout the nineteenth century, as Kosrae became an increasingly popular base for pirates and New England whalers, who brought with them tobacco and whisky—and infectious diseases. By 1910 only 300 Kosraeans had survived the Western imports of smallpox, measles, influenza, and sexually transmitted diseases.

James Ned, a geneticist at the University of Michigan Medical School who died in 2000, hypothesized in a 1962 article on diabetes that under conditions of scarcity natural selection weeds out people unable to store food efficiently in their bodies, and that a "thrifty genotype" encourages the conversion of calories into body fat. He suggested that this mechanism was necessary for survival during periods of extreme stress and famine that would otherwise ravage a population. Most populations are assumed to have some variation on this genotype, but it is likely that peoples whose evolution was punctuated by a number of particularly harrowing events developed the most-effective versions. In Kosrae, where weather and disease wiped out 90 percent of the population, this effect must have been profound. The very genes presumed to have protected islanders from their history are now believed to be predisposing them to life-threatening illnesses. . . .

Writing in *Nature* in 1992, Jared Diamond, a professor of physiology at the UCLA Medical School, suggested that the populations of Western industrial nations had already to some extent weeded out the thrifty genotype, keeping diabetes and obesity below the levels now common in Micronesia. "Before modern medicine made [diabetes] more manageable," he wrote, "genetically susceptible Europeans would have been gradually eliminated, bringing [diabetes] to its present [relatively] low frequency." Diamond and others have suggested that some human populations, notably those that evolved in regions of Europe, may have developed a relative resistance to certain noncommunicable diseases just as they did to some infectious diseases—through natural

> *"It is likely that billions of human beings are genetically programmed to get fat—and sick—when exposed to the Western lifestyle."*

selection over centuries of relatively sustained plenty. Given the burgeoning rates of obesity and diabetes in the United States and other industrialized nations, this seems surprising, until one considers that rates among the most susceptible peoples—Pacific Islanders such as Native Hawaiians, Samoans, and Nauruans—are higher still. Indeed, all measures indicate that the greatest impact of obesity-related disorders will continue to be in newly industrialized and developing nations in Asia, Africa, the Caribbean, Latin America, and the Indian and Pacific Oceans which historically had an unstable food supply.

A New Health Crisis in the Developing World

The World Health Organization recently described overeating as the "fastest growing form of malnourishment" in the world. For the first time in history the number of people worldwide who are both overweight and malnourished, estimated at 1.1 billion, equals the number who are underweight and malnourished. Obesity rates in China have quadrupled in the past decade, and obesity in the urban middle class in India is epidemic. In Colombia 41 percent of adults are overweight. The global spread of diet-linked disease presents one of the greatest medical challenges of the twenty-first century.

But when I spoke with agricultural and business leaders in Micronesia, it was clear that a concerted government effort to fight noncommunicable disease was not likely on these islands. I heard repeatedly that health was a matter of willpower and individual effort, and that government could do nothing to curb the public taste for imports. The fact that many state legislators in Micronesia are also food importers was never mentioned—nor were the particulars of auto importation in a tiny country already overrun with cars.

Father Francis Hezel, a Jesuit priest from Buffalo, New York, who has spent more than three decades teaching and writing in Micronesia, said that even people in power are reluctant to speak out. "You can enter any clinic and smell the decaying limbs, rotted by diabetes," he told me. "But many people here are beholden to the government. They don't want to rock the boat." In Micronesia—as in much of the world, particularly the developing world—it is more profitable for authorities to encourage overconsumption than to discourage it. The Worldwatch Institute reported last year that approximately four of the five McDonald's restaurants that opened every day in 1997 were outside the United States. In its 1998 annual report the Coca-Cola Company described Africa as "a land of opportunity."

Obesity, diabetes, and other manifestations of New World syndrome can, like infectious diseases, be contained. In Singapore the nationwide Trim and Fit Scheme, which began in 1992, has cut childhood obesity by up to 50 percent. And in Hawaii, Terry Shintani and colleagues at the Waianae Coast Comprehensive Health Center have shown long-term health benefits from a program emphasizing a return to traditional local foods.

We spotted a glimmer of progress in Micronesia, though not in the Western-style wellness programs. One of our hosts, a hospital administrator, told us that he neither farmed nor fished but did enjoy playing basketball, and that he would sometimes jog rather than drive to the high school gym to play. As a result of this regimen he had lost a significant amount of weight, and avoided some of the health problems suffered by his more sedentary compatriots. Basketball, he said, was catching on quickly in Kosrae, as was baseball. "Imports made us sick," he said. "Now maybe imports will help us get well."

However nice the thought, increasing amounts of junk food are being shipped into Kosrae from the West, food importers say, and the island is about to import television programming. Kosraeans will be able to come home, open a few cans of Spam, switch on the tube, and kick back for the evening. It is then that they will truly be able to live—and die—in the manner of their Western benefactors.

It is likely that billions of human beings are genetically primed to get fat—and sick—when exposed to the Western lifestyle. Exportation of this lifestyle is an inevitable consequence of globalism, but its health risks need not be. Curbing the international obesity epidemic is as tough a problem as any now facing public-health officials. But given the lessons of Kosrae, it is worth taking very seriously.

Abusive Child Labor Is a Problem in Developing Nations

by John J. Tierney Jr.

About the author: *John J. Tierney Jr. is faculty chairman of the Institute of World Politics, a private graduate school of statecraft and national security in Washington, D.C.*

To most Americans the problem of exploitative child labor disappeared generations ago with the passage of child labor laws and the elimination of dangerous "sweatshop" conditions. But the problem of child exploitation—an iniquitous subset of a much larger economically and socially legitimate and family-friendly culture of child work—is a living reality in many areas of the developing world, and the issue has commanded growing attention in the Western world.

As Senator Joseph Biden (D-Delaware) told a U.S. Department of Labor hearing in 1997,

> In an age of computers, fiber optics, and space travel, it is easy to forget that in many parts of the world—including our own backyard—children are sold into servitude, chained to machines, and forced to work under the most dangerous and unsanitary conditions. For most American consumers, the plight of these children has been as distant as a novel by Charles Dickens—not a present-day reality.

Some of that changed in 1998, however, when television personality Kathie Lee Gifford was accused of permitting the exploitation of children in Honduran factories that manufactured clothes bearing her designer label. Gifford denied the charge and testified against child abuse before Congress, thus defusing the issue at the time.

Yet most Americans still find the idea of abusing children for profit repugnant—notwithstanding the long tradition of child labor in U.S. industries and farms during the eighteenth and nineteenth centuries, a time when America it-self was a developing country. A survey conducted by Marymount University found that more than three out of four Americans would avoid shopping at stores if they were aware that the goods sold were made by exploitative and abusive child labor.

The issue also reverberated against various U.S. sporting goods manufactur-ers, including Reebok, after allegations of abusive child labor conditions in soc-cer ball factories in Pakistan. These charges forced an overhaul of the soccer in-dustry's approach to the child labor issue. Three concrete steps were undertaken by the industry in mid-1996: Subcontracting was eliminated, cooperation with the government was instituted, and monitoring of the soccer industry com-menced.

In a 1998 hearing, Tom Cove, vice president of the Sporting Goods Manufac-turers Association, told a Labor Department hearing that "I am proud to report today that the U.S. soccer industry, with the help of many essential partners, has been true to all three of these explicit commitments."

A Need for Regulation

These are positive steps and reflect a mounting awareness that child labor abuse is a growing international problem that needs regulation. Senator Tom Harkin (D-Iowa) is probably the nation's top lawmaker in this area. His Child-Labor-Free Consumer Information Act of 1997 would institute a voluntary la-beling system for certifying that sporting goods and wearing apparel were made without child labor abuse.

"We need that," Harkin told a government panel, "because today the price we see for an item in a store—like a soccer ball or tennis shoes or a shirt or a blouse—tells us how much we have to pay for it. But it doesn't tell us how much someone else had to pay to make it."

The International Labor Organization (ILO) estimates that at least 250 mil-lion children between the ages of 5 and 14 are working, mostly in the develop-ing world. About half of these work full time, while tens of millions work under conditions defined as "exploitative and harmful." The majority of the 250 mil-lion are found in Asia (61 percent), followed by Africa (32 percent) and Latin America and the Caribbean (7 percent).

Until recently, child labor was not a widely recognized global concern. It was not until 1993 that the U.S. De-

> *"At least 250 million children between the ages of 5 and 14 are working, mostly in the developing world."*

partment of Labor, under congressional mandate, began researching and docu-menting the issue. International public attention regarding child labor has grown steadily over the past several years, however, and has provoked a global discussion of the problem and possible solutions.

In the spring of 1998, for example, over 1,400 Non-Government Organizations (NGOs) showed their concern over the plight of child workers by supporting the Global March Against Child Labor, a six-month-long march around the world. Large international conferences held in Stockholm, Amsterdam, and Oslo demonstrated support for ending abusive child labor.

According to the ILO (Convention No. 138), the term child labor generally refers to any economic activity performed by a person under the age of 15. Not all of this, of course, is harmful or exploitative. Certain types of work, such as apprenticeship or family-related chores after school, can be a formative and constructive learning experience. But the type of child labor that has become the focus of international concern is the abusive, unhealthy, commercial exploitation of children that interferes with their education.

ILO statistics have listed the majority of working children as involved in agriculture, fishing, forestry, and hunting (61 percent). The remainder work in manufacturing (8 percent); retail and trade services (8 percent); community and personal services (7 percent); transport, storage, and communications (4 percent); construction (2 percent); and mining and quarrying (1 percent).

Agriculture. Payment based upon seasonal harvesting and seeding provides an incentive for parents to supplement their income dramatically by bringing their children into the fields with them at peak times. These children often start very young, since picking and digging can be performed as early as six or seven years of age.

> *"In Brazil, close to 150,000 children work in severe heat during the six-month orange harvest season for as long as 12 hours a day."*

In some countries, children comprise a significant percentage of the agricultural workforce. In parts of Mexico, this reaches 30 percent. In Kenya, it can top 50 percent during peak periods. In Brazil, close to 150,000 children work in severe heat during the six-month orange harvest season for as long as 12 hours a day.

Hazards in agriculture include sharp and unwieldy tools, bites from insects and snakes, unsafe vehicles, and regular exposure to toxic substances such as chemical fertilizers and pesticides.

Fishing. In the global fishing industry, children are employed to dive for fish, to work on docks or boats, or to peel and clean the catch. They often spend long hours in the water without protective gear and face hazards such as drowning, skin diseases, and shark attacks.

Manufacturing. Most child labor in manufacturing occurs in small workshops or in home-based work. Hazardous conditions include dangerous and unsupervised machinery, long hours, lack of protective gear, intense heat, poor lighting, bad ventilation, loud noise, and exposure to toxic substances.

Mining and quarrying. Child labor is common in small-scale mining and stone quarrying throughout the developing world. The number of children in this sector is relatively small, but the percentage of injuries is high. ILO statistics list one in every five girls and one in every six boys employed in mines and quarries as being affected by illness or injury.

Services. Children throughout the developing world work in a number of service-related tasks. Over 300,000 Filipino children work as domestic servants. In Bangladesh, a survey found that 24 percent of domestics were less than 10 years old. A study in Brazil found nearly 260,000 domestics between 10 and 14. In Peru, 80 percent of domestics are girls.

> *"The countries with the highest illiteracy rates, lowest school enrollments, and the worst nutritional deficiencies employ the highest percentage of children."*

Such children typically perform household chores, run errands, provide child care, clean, do laundry, and cook. They often work long hours, receive little pay, and have few days off. In many cases, they receive harsh treatment from their employers.

Child prostitution is also common, particularly in Asia. Thailand, for example, has earned an international reputation for this offense, with thousands of girls from China and Southeast Asia regularly being kidnapped and sold to brothels in Bangkok and other Thai locales. This practice also takes place throughout the major urban centers of India, Pakistan, Africa, and Latin America.

Other service-related child labor is found in myriad occupations, including street vending, hotel and restaurant work, car repair, and construction.

The Culture of Child Labor

To combat exploitative child labor, it is necessary to consider carefully its various forms, to distinguish between legitimate work and illegitimate exploitation, and to appreciate the developmental and cultural context in which child labor exists. This may be difficult in a prosperous America, but there was, in fact, a time when children worked long and hard hours in the factories, stores, and farmlands of the young United States.

It is also important to remember that the gradual erosion of child labor in the United States occurred within the context of political liberty and free-market economics. This system remains the only reliable model for the elimination of the conditions that cause child labor in the first place.

There is wide consensus that harmful child labor is directly related to poverty. The countries with the highest illiteracy rates, lowest school enrollments, and the worst nutritional deficiencies employ the highest percentage of children.

Beyond this level of generality, however, the phenomenon becomes more complex. Poverty is a general cause but far from the only one. Child labor is also associated with cultural traditions, lack of educational opportunities, and low levels of development. Imposing solutions outside the context of such social, economic, and cultural conditions has the potential to worsen the problem. Unless some alternative can be found for working children and their families, for example, many children dismissed from work will be forced to fend for themselves or will only adopt more hazardous forms of activity, including crime.

The American and Western revulsion over child labor is, in fact, by no means a universal concern. In some countries, child labor is defended as necessary for economic viability, often for survival itself. A major study by the Canadian International Development Agency, for example, noted: "The causes of child labor are varied. Poverty is the main but not the only cause. . . . Work is a matter of survival for children of poor families."

The social context, therefore, has to be taken into account alongside economic conditions. Lack of awareness, desperation, and indifference drive the problem in poor countries where children are used for perceived advantages. For one thing, children require less pay than adults. Another cause is the "nimble finger" argument—that is, that only children can perform certain delicate tasks. Child labor is also considered less troublesome than that of adults, because children are more docile.

Many developing countries resent the intrusion of the wealthy and industrial West, under the guise of "human rights," into their national workplace. Shabbin Jamal, for example, an adviser to Pakistan's Ministry of Labor, has deplored the Western world's "double standard" in failing to recognize what he sees as an economic need.

"Westerners conveniently forget their own shameful histories when they come here," he noted recently. "Europeans addressed slavery and child labor only after they became prosperous. Pakistan has only now entered an era of economic stability that will allow us to expand our horizons and address social concerns."

Indeed, the family and national need for child labor is regarded as a necessity in most developing nations. Healthy labor, under supervised conditions,

> *"The family and national need for child labor is regarded as a necessity in most developing nations."*

can also be productive and rewarding in the growth of a child. Save the Children, an international alliance formed to protect the rights of working children, has been very explicit that the goal should be to eradicate exploitation rather than child labor itself. Calling blanket bans on work by children "dangerous," the group has also recognized that "work can be a way of children gaining skills and increasing their choices."

Thus, many analysts believe, reformers should keep in mind that the goal should be to end abuse and hazardous conditions, not necessarily the labor itself. Emotional responses, as occurred regarding Bangladesh, must be avoided. In this case, the United States threatened to ban all goods coming from Bangladesh garment makers who employed children, prompting the factory owners to fire all employees under 14. Deprived of their much-needed income, these children had to take on harmful and less lucrative work, with most of the girls resorting to prostitution.

The lesson here is that honest labor can be productive and profitable for young and old alike, and that employing children is an economic necessity for millions who cannot afford even the simplest of luxuries. Under proper and supervised conditions, children can advance their skills and range of career choices while helping to support their families. The issue is the condition of the workplace, not the work itself—but the whole issue is still huge and growing, with much left to be resolved.

Need for Teeth in Child Labor Laws

The elimination of exploitative child labor has recently become a worldwide priority. Most countries now have laws prohibiting work by children under a certain age and regulating working conditions for older children. But the problem for the moment is not the lack of legislation but its general inefficiency, leniency, and inconsistency. As a 1998 U.S. Department of Labor report stated, "Inadequate enforcement of child labor laws is a common problem throughout the world. Not all labor ministries are institutionally capable of enforcing child labor laws."

Both ILO Convention No. 138 and Article 32 of the UN Convention on the Rights of the Child call on countries to establish a minimum wage, to regulate hours and working conditions, and to provide appropriate penalties and sanctions when such rules are not met. Many nations have ratified one or both of these conventions, but legislation and enforcement mechanisms often fall short of these standards.

A dramatic breakthrough took place in June 1999, however, when the ILO unanimously adopted a convention that requires all ratifying countries to "take immediate and effective measures" to eliminate the worst cases of child abuse. The U.S. Senate approved the treaty on November 5, 1999, and President Clinton signed it into law during the World Trade Organization conference in December, making the United States the first industrial nation to do so.

The United States is also the largest contributor to the ILO's program to eliminate child labor, having increased its contribution from $3 million to $30 million for fiscal year 1999.

But the "war" on abusive child labor will require time and patience. Deputy Undersecretary of Labor Andrew Samet has noted that the issue is "in a sense, a time-bound question . . . solvable within the next 15 years." This may be an optimistic forecast, but it's also an objective worth pursuing.

Air Pollution Is a Serious Problem in Developing Nations

by Katherine Bolt, Susmita Dasgupta, Kiran Pandey, and David Wheeler

About the authors: *Katherine Bolt, Susmita Dasgupta, Kiran Pandey, and David Wheeler are members of the World Bank's Environment Department and Development Research Group in Washington, D.C.*

Polluted air is a major health hazard in many parts of the world, but it is particularly troublesome in some developing countries, where regulations governing air quality have traditionally been lax or nonexistent. The international health community currently believes suspended particulate matter—commonly known as dust—to be the most damaging among widely measured air pollutants. Ambient concentrations of particulates in many cities of the developing world routinely exceed the World Health Organization safety standard by a factor of three or more.

Particulate air pollution is a complex mixture of small and large particles of varying origin and chemical composition. Over time, health research on air pollution has narrowed its focus from all particles to small particles less than 10 microns in diameter and, most recently, to particles whose diameters are less than 2.5 microns.

Large particles usually contain dust and smoke from industrial processes, construction, agriculture, and road traffic, as well as plant pollen and other natural sources. Smaller particles generally originate from combustion of fossil fuels. These particles include soot from vehicle exhaust, which is often coated with chemical contaminants or metals, and fine sulfate and nitrate aerosols that form when sulfur dioxide and nitrogen oxide emissions condense in the atmosphere. The largest sources of fine particles are coal-fired power plants and motor vehicles. Small particles are more dangerous because they can penetrate deep into the lungs, settling in areas where natural clearance mechanisms, like coughing, cannot remove them. The constituent elements in small particles also tend to be more chemically active and therefore more damaging.

Recent epidemiological studies have reported that exposure to particulates, particularly small particulates, is strongly associated with respiratory illness and death. For urban residents in Latin America, some estimates suggest that particulates cause 65 million days of illness each year. A 1996 study finds that particulate pollution has inflicted serious health damage on the 4.8 million inhabitants of Santiago, Chile, a city with particularly poor air quality. Other research indicates that air pollution in Jakarta, Indonesia, is responsible for some 1,400 deaths, 49,000 emergency-room visits, and 600,000 asthma attacks per year. Health effects of exposure to particulates range in severity from coughing and bronchitis to heart disease and lung cancer.

> *"Particulate air pollution kills about 750,000 people annually in developing regions, with over 300,000 in China alone."*

Numerous studies have indicated that there is no "critical threshold" that governs safe exposure levels to particulate pollution. Damage increases with exposure, starting at very low concentration levels. As research on damage from particulate pollution has accumulated, policymakers in developing countries have begun modifying their traditional concern about diverting resources to pollution control when poverty, illiteracy, and infant mortality are still major problems. Their past hesitation has, in part, resulted from uncertainty about local pollution levels, but recently, measurement of particulate pollution has become much more common.

New Evidence

The new monitoring data from developing countries are enabling researchers to provide much more detailed information about the scope and severity of particulate pollution. Using an econometric model calibrated to the latest data, our research team at the World Bank has recently developed estimates of ambient concentrations for more than 3,200 cities. The model incorporates a number of factors, including population density, economic activity, fuel use, and meteorological conditions.

The data show that average concentrations in East Asia (mostly China) and South Asia (mostly India) are about four times higher than average concentrations in member nations of the Organisation for Economic Co-operation and Development (OECD), while average concentrations are about twice as high in Sub-Saharan Africa, Eastern Europe, the Middle East, and Latin America. These estimates suggest that a majority of city dwellers in developing countries face significant health risks from particulate pollution.

Using the latest research on the link between particulate pollution and health damage, we have extended our analysis to estimate damage to human health as well as impact on economic activity. We estimate that particulate air pollution kills about 750,000 people annually in developing regions, with over 300,000 in China alone.

For the world as a whole, developing regions account for over 90 percent of mortality, morbidity, hospital visits, and lost working days. Translating these numbers into economic losses, four developing regions have estimated annual gross domestic product reductions greater than 1.5 percent—a substantial loss in countries whose annual income growth has averaged around 5 percent in recent years. China suffers close to half of the total damage from air pollution in developing countries.

Recent Trends

Fortunately, developing countries have not been ignoring this problem. . . . All the figures suggest substantial reductions in particulate pollution. Despite China's poverty and rapid industrialization, its major urban areas have experienced a significant decline in suspended particulates. During the period from 1987 to 1995, the average concentration fell from nearly 500 micrograms per cubic meter to just over 300. While the latter measure is still far above the traditional World Health Organization standard for clean air, a 40-percent decline in pollution has undoubtedly saved many lives in China.

After rising in the early 1990s, Mexico City's percentage of suspended particulate readings above

"As [developing nations'] income and education levels improve, they will control pollution more strictly."

standards fell to historical lows in the latter part of the decade. In Cubatao, Brazil, the average concentration fell from 155 mg/m³ in 1984 to around 80 mg/m³ in 1998. While equivalent measures are still lacking in many developing countries, these trends provide hopeful evidence that pollution can be substantially reduced when the political will and supporting institutions are present.

Contribution of Research

Numerous studies during the past decade have contributed to this positive trend, both in calling attention to the problem and suggesting potentially effective approaches to dealing with it. Medical research has demonstrated that many of the health effects of particulate pollution—such as bronchitis, tightness in the chest, and wheezing—are short-term and can be reversed if exposure to air pollution declines.

Several recent benefit-cost analyses have made a persuasive case for stricter air-pollution control. In China, for instance, a recent study has shown that the economic returns on investments in pollution abatement would justify significant tightening of regulations. Similar studies in Brazil and Indonesia have produced similar conclusions.

Recent policy research has also suggested a broad scope for improving air quality in developing countries, for several reasons. First, communities in developing countries are neither passive agents nor are they focused exclusively on material gain. Empowered with good information about the benefits and costs of environmental protection, they will act to protect their own interests. As their income and education levels improve, they will control pollution more strictly.

Second, consumers and investors assign significant value to environmental performance, and, if they are well informed, their market decisions will provide powerful incentives for reducing pollution. On both counts, the most plausible long-run forecast is for rising, not falling, environmental quality. While this news is good for developing countries, adjustment to a cleaner world will require significant commitment to building new regulatory institutions and programs. Numerous examples demonstrate that such programs have already made an important difference.

Many developing nations have already adopted ambitious ambient air-quality standards for suspended particulates, . . . but attaining these standards for stationary pollution sources such as power plants and factories will require more attention to policies in the following categories.

Targeted Enforcement

Among stationary pollution sources, a few facilities are generally responsible for most of the pollution. As a consequence, it is possible to reduce emissions significantly by targeting regulatory monitoring and enforcement on those dominant sources. Furthermore, large polluters can often respond to regulation more readily because they have more skilled personnel, the resources to buy and run pollution control equipment, and the ability to spread administrative costs over many units of activity.

A good illustration of such targeting is provided by the case of FEEMA, the pollution-control agency of Rio de Janeiro State in Brazil. FEEMA program analysts have ranked several thousand factories according to their contribution to the overall volume and risks of local air and water pollution. The agency has assigned factories to categories A, B, and C according to plant size, and their analysis suggests that 60 percent of the state's serious industrial pollution could be controlled by targeting only 50 factories in the A group. Controlling pollution from 150 plants in the B group would eliminate another 20 percent of the total. Targeting the first 300 plants in the C group, which numbers in the thousands, would cut 10 percent more pollution.

> *"Pollution has been significantly reduced by programs that provide accessible information to the public about specific polluters and pollution damages."*

Targeting larger plants seems to have impressive potential for reducing pollution, but will it also save lives? Large factories have taller stacks, so their emissions are less concentrated and less dangerous to nearby residents, but according to a recent study in Brazil, large plants remain the source of most deaths because the sheer volume of their emissions simply overwhelms the higher per-unit emissions hazard from smaller plants. Thus, the targeting strategy adopted by Brazilian regulatory agencies has great potential for reducing pollution while making the most of scarce administrative resources.

Pollution Charges

Notable inroads against pollution have been made where environmental agencies in developing countries have moved away from traditional command-and-control regulatory policies toward economic instruments such as pollution-charge systems. These systems apply economic incentives by charging polluters for every unit of their emissions.

Pollution charges have proven feasible and effective in developing countries, and they have been implemented successfully in China, Colombia, Malaysia, and Philippines. The results have shown clearly that firms' managers opt for significant pollution-control measures when they face steep, regular payments for emissions. Pollution charges not only cut emissions but generate public revenue as well—which in turn can support local efforts to control pollution.

The most impressive example is the pollution-charge system of China, which is by far the largest in the developing world. In response to China's enormous problems, almost all of China's counties and cities have implemented charges for air and water pollution, solid and radioactive waste, and noise. Some 300,000 factories have paid for their emissions, and more than 19 billion yuan ($US 2.3 billion) has been collected. About 80 percent of the funds have been used to finance pollution prevention and control, accounting for about 15 percent of total investment in these activities.

As of 1995, the levy had financed or cofinanced about 220,000 pollution-control projects, with abatement capacity equivalent to 16 billion tons of waste water, 4 billion cubic meters of waste gas, 70 million tons of solid waste, and 19,000 noise sources. The Chinese charge system has been criticized on the grounds that plants are charged only for pollution in excess of standards, that the charge is levied only on the single air or water pollutant that most seriously violates the standard, and that charges are often too low to induce abatement to the legally required level. But despite various weaknesses, the system has proven highly potent in fighting pollution. Recent research has shown that each 10 percent increase in the air pollution charge has cut particulate pollution by about 4 percent. This, coupled with other regulatory measures, has actually reduced air pollution in many cities during a decade in which industrial output has more than doubled.

Emissions trading is another innovative and potentially cost-effective economic instrument for controlling pollution. Under this system, all stationary emission sources are required to acquire permits to pollute, and each permit specifies how much the pollution source is allowed to emit. The control authority issues the number of permits needed to produce the desired emission level, and any emission by a source in excess of its permitted amount leads to severe monetary sanctions. Under this pollution-control regime, the permits are freely transferable among firms; firms that keep emissions below their permitted amounts can sell excess permits to firms that find it more difficult or costly to reduce pollution.

"The motor vehicle fleet is growing rapidly in most developing countries and accounts for a significant portion of air pollution."

Numerous emissions-trading systems have been established in the OECD countries. In the developing world, Chile has adopted emissions trading as part of its effort to control air pollution in Santiago. The system was introduced in 1992 for large, stationary polluters. Allocation of emissions permits is proportional to the scale of activities that generate waste gases, and permits are freely tradable across facilities.

Experience to date suggests that emissions-trading systems engender a number of operational complexities under the conditions present in many developing countries. First, a complete inventory of pollution sources and their emissions is needed before the system can be instituted. Second, emissions trading can be hindered by the cost of searching for trading partners, which can contribute to a firm's uncertainty about cost-effective pollution control measures. Meanwhile, trading can create local pollution "hotspots" when large polluters in one area buy emissions permits from other polluters that are far away. Controlling for such spatial considerations is possible, but it inevitably increases transactions difficulties and reduces the cost-effectiveness of the system.

Public Information

During the past few years, pollution has been significantly reduced by programs that provide accessible information to the public about specific polluters and pollution damages. Such programs work because they improve the ability of local communities to protect themselves, they help national regulators enforce decent environmental standards, and they allow market agents to reward clean firms and punish heavy polluters.

The story of a pioneering Indonesian program illustrates the efficacy of public information in action. Starting in the 1980s, BAPEDAL, the Indonesian national pollution-control agency, tried to control factory pollution by enforcing traditional regulatory standards. But enforcement was weak because the regulatory budget was limited and the courts were plagued by corruption. Meanwhile, industrial output was growing at over 10 percent annually, and by the mid-

1990s, the government was becoming concerned about the risk of severe damage from pollution.

In response, BAPEDAL decided to initiate a program that rated and publicly disclosed the environmental performance of Indonesian factories. The agency hoped that the resulting pressure would provide a low-cost way to promote compliance with regulations and create new incentives for managers to adopt cleaner technologies. The Indonesian initiative is called the Program for Pollution Control, Evaluation and Rating (PROPER). Under PROPER, BAPEDAL rates factories' environmental performance and publicly awards a color code to each polluter. Black denotes factories that make no attempt to control pollution and cause severe damage, while red denotes those that have some pollution control but fall short of compliance. Factories that adhere to national standards receive a blue rating, and those whose emission controls and production and waste-management procedures significantly exceed national standards receive a green label. World-class performers receive a gold ranking.

In the pilot phase of PROPER, which began in early 1995, BAPEDAL rated water pollution from 187 plants. Some 18 months after full disclosure, considerable reduction was evident in the black and red categories, and compliant plants, originally one-third of the sample, constituted over half. A similar pilot disclosure program in Philippines, ECOWATCH, increased the number of compliant firms by 50 percent 18 months after disclosure.

After witnessing the success of such initiatives, international institutions such as the World Bank have begun supporting public disclosure in collaborative programs with environmental agencies in China, India, Thailand, Vietnam, Mexico, Colombia, and elsewhere.

Controlling Mobile Sources

The motor vehicle fleet is growing rapidly in most developing countries and accounts for a significant portion of air pollution. The relatively small size and mobility of vehicles requires a different policy mix for three main reasons. First, mobility and the possibility of resale mean that, over their working lifetimes, individual vehicles may be operated in a variety of urban and rural settings. Such flexibility makes it very difficult to tailor vehicle-based regulations to particular local circumstances.

"Without sustained political commitment . . . and strong financial support from the international aid community, the air in the developing world will remain deadly."

Second, mobile sources are far more numerous than stationary sources, so enforcement is difficult and costly. And third, many vehicles are operated by individuals who have little technical knowledge. This makes it more likely that emission control will deteriorate over time, because of a lack of consistent maintenance. To counter such difficulties, programs to control vehicular emissions have ventured beyond traditional pollution regulation to activities as diverse as land-use planning, demand management, traffic management, vehicle emissions standards, and cleaner fuels.

In the OECD, urban development based on "motorization" has resulted in vehicle-dependent economies with serious mobile-source pollution problems. Better results are obtained by urban-growth strategies that emphasize settlement corridors served by efficient public transit. Curitiba, Brazil, has pioneered this approach for developing countries. For maximum effect, it must be introduced before urban sprawl and population dispersal undermine the cost-effectiveness of public transit services.

To reduce vehicular pollution, policymakers have also used a variety of demand-management instruments such as fuel taxes, regulatory restrictions on driving, parking fees, urban zoning, and subsidies for public transportation. Among these instruments, fuel taxes have been particularly popular. Fuel combustion causes vehicular pollution, so such taxes reduce pollution by reducing the demand for—and consumption of—motor fuels.

The appeal of fuel taxes lies partly in their familiarity, since all countries intervene to some extent in fuel markets. Another appeal is their administrative simplicity, since collection requires little or no monitoring. On the other hand, general fuel taxes do not address spatial and temporal pollution problems effectively. Attempts to vary taxes across regions inevitably generate illegal "parallel markets," and vehicle fuel storage capacity undermines any attempt to increase taxes during hours of peak congestion and pollution.

To counter these weaknesses, fuel taxes are frequently complemented by more-direct measures such as driving restrictions, charging commuters a fee for driving during times of peak congestion, parking fees, and public-transport subsidies. Such measures can be counter productive if they are not well thought out. For example, Mexico City has attempted to complement the Mexican fuel tax with a program that uses vehicles' license numbers to ban them from use on one day each week. Unfortunately, city residents have evaded the program by purchasing second vehicles that are old, cheap, and highly polluting. As a consequence, this program may actually have worsened air quality.

Santiago, Chile, has a similar program that restricts vehicle use during high-pollution periods, but it avoids the Mexican problem by applying the measure only to old vehicles that do not have effective emission controls.

Traffic Management

The slow operating speeds of motor vehicles in major cities of the developing world result in high fuel consumption and significant air pollution. In this context, new proposals for improved urban management stress improved traffic engineering, traffic control, and traffic enforcement, and grant priority access to buses and other high-occupancy vehicles. Other suggested improvements include strict limitation of parking spaces when public transit is available and stricter regulation of available on-street parking.

There is essentially unanimous agreement that stricter emissions standards should be reflected in the design of new vehicles and progressively tightened to avoid prohibitive cost escalation in the short run. Numerous experiments have shown that testing programs administered independently of vehicle manufacturers can help reduce emissions. Considerable pollution reduction has also accompanied the mandated conversion of urban high-occupancy vehicle fleets to compressed natural gas.

Dust's Death Toll

Recent research has persuasively documented the extent of air pollution damage in the cities of the developing world. During the past decade, as many as 10 million people may have died prematurely from particulate air pollution generated by stationary and mobile sources. At the same time, health-related economic losses may have neutralized a significant part of the income growth that developing countries have managed to achieve.

Fortunately, policymakers are no longer ignoring this problem. In several major industrialized countries of the developing world, a variety of policy measures have significantly reduced air pollution over the past 10 years. Others, however, have barely begun the struggle. The more-effective nations have introduced policy instruments that have significantly reduced deadly air pollution. More widespread implementation of these measures can save millions of lives and prevent huge economic losses during the coming decade. But without sustained political commitment from domestic policymakers and strong financial support from the international aid community, the air in the developing world will remain deadly.

Infectious Disease Is a Serious Problem in Developing Nations

by Kevin Finneran

About the author: *Kevin Finneran is editor-in-chief of* Issues in Science and Technology *magazine.*

The horror of [the] September 11 [terrorist attacks on America] is difficult to absorb. We all looked in disbelief as the tape of the buildings collapsing was played over and over and over again. We watched thinking that if we saw it often enough perhaps we could feel the magnitude of the loss. For more than three months the *New York Times* ran biographical sketches of the people who were killed that day in an effort to help us slowly come to understand the magnitude of this mind-numbing tragedy.

On November 2, the Department of State in cooperation with the National Academies sponsored an all-day meeting on a human disaster of even greater magnitude—the spread of infectious disease in the developing world. The day that 3,000 people died at the Trade Towers and the Pentagon, more than 8,000 people died of AIDS, 5,000 people died of tuberculosis, and several thousand more died of malaria. Of course, these deaths are different, because disease is not murder. Nobody wanted these deaths to occur, no one made them happen.

Yet these deaths are not exactly the same as deaths from disease in the developed world. With the exception of AIDS, infectious diseases are not taking the lives of young people in the rich countries, because most diseases can be prevented or treated relatively inexpensively, and even AIDS is being contained by prevention efforts. In Africa infectious diseases are the cause of almost 70 percent of all deaths. What makes the enormous toll of death in the developing world not just the way of all flesh is that we know very well what has to be done to prevent most of these deaths. But we don't act. And by not acting, we know that we are signing an early death warrant for tens of millions of people.

The nation's leaders are not insensitive to the seriousness of this neglect. Even as the nation reeled in shock from the events of September 11, Senator Bill Frist (R-Tenn.) and State Department science advisor Norman Neureiter told participants at the meeting how important it is to address global health problems. Secretary of State Colin Powell was scheduled to speak but was called away to meet with congressional leaders. His prepared remarks, which were read at the meeting, indicate that he understands the severity of the problem and is looking for ways to take effective action.

The Scope of the Problem

The most comprehensive description of the problem and what will be needed to fix it came from Barry Bloom, dean of Harvard University's School of Public Health. Using data from the World Health Organization (WHO), he painted a devastating picture of human suffering and economic disaster.

Tuberculosis infects 8.4 million people per year and results in 2 million deaths, virtually all in the developing world. About one-third of deaths of AIDS patients in Africa are attributed to tuberculosis. It results in $1 billion in lost income from people too sick to work, $11 billion in future lost income from those who die, and $4 billion in diagnosis and treatment costs. Malaria infects 400 million–900 million people a year and results in 0.7–2.7 million deaths. More than 36 million people are living with AIDS, and 25 million of them are in sub-Saharan Africa. Of the roughly 3 million AIDS-related deaths that occurred last year, about 2.4 million were in sub-Saharan Africa. Of the 5.3 million new infections in 2000, about 3.8 million were in sub-Saharan Africa.

"More than 36 million people are living with AIDS, and 25 million of them are in sub-Saharan Africa."

The pain and suffering caused by infectious disease do not end with the infected individuals and their families. Bloom explained that the economic repercussions touch everyone in the developing countries and deepen the cycle of poverty that is the breeding ground of disease. Too many people are dying before they can use their education to contribute to the society through work. WHO estimates that the short life expectancy in the least developed countries (49 years) compared to the 77 years of people in the industrialized world results in an annual economic growth deficit of 1.6 percent, which becomes an enormous difference over time.

Opportunities for Action

Although these numbers are daunting enough to lead to despair, Bloom sees plenty of opportunity for effective action, even with AIDS. He cites a vivid example of how effective prevention efforts can be. In 1990, AIDS infection rates were about 1 percent in South Africa and slightly lower in Thailand. Thai officials recognized how devastating an AIDS epidemic could be and instituted an ambitious AIDS education and prevention program. In 2000, HIV prevalence in Thailand had increased, but it was still below 3 percent. By contrast, South Africa did little to control the spread of the disease, and the infection rate is now close to 25 percent.

The prospects for improvement are much better with malaria and tuberculosis, because we have effective vaccines and treatments. The solution is simple—money. Bloom explains that a billion people live on less than $1 a day. In the 44 countries with av-

> *"The humanitarian and economic reasons to take action against global infectious disease have never been more compelling."*

erage per capita income of less than $500 per year, the average health expenditure is $12 per person per year. Bloom has worked with other public health experts to help WHO develop a plan that would dramatically decrease the incidence of deadly infectious diseases at a cost that the developed countries could easily afford.

The experience of countries that have implemented programs for the early detection and treatment of tuberculosis indicates that extending this effort worldwide would cost about $900 million per year and result in an estimated economic return of $6 billion per year through increased worker production. With malaria the key is more aggressive prevention efforts to stop mosquitoes from stinging people. Actions would include increased insecticide treatment of existing mosquito netting, the purchase of additional nets and insecticide, increased spraying of breeding areas, and chemoprophylaxis for children. Economic analysis indicates that a 10 percent reduction in the incidence of malaria could lead to a 0.3 percent increase in annual economic growth. Bloom estimates that implementing an AIDS prevention program such as the one used in Thailand would yield an economic return of 37–55 percent through averted income losses and medical expenditures.

A comprehensive program for addressing the related economic and health problems of developing countries was released by the WHO-appointed Commission on Macroeconomics and Health in December 2001. The report (available online at www.who.int) contains a detailed analysis of how annual expenditures of about $34 per capita aimed at reducing the harm caused by HIV/AIDS, malaria, tuberculosis, childhood infectious diseases, maternal and perinatal conditions, micronutrient deficiencies, and tobacco-related illnesses could prevent 8 million premature deaths per year. Money for the program would come from increased spending by the developing countries themselves and a significant increase in support from the wealthy countries. Donor spending would reach $27 billion during 2007 and $38 billion in 2015. About a third of the donor funding would go to the Global Fund to Fight AIDS, Tuberculosis, and Malaria. Estimated economic benefits would be in the hundreds of billions and would be reflected not only in better health but also in more robust economic growth that would eventually make it possible to reduce the need for assistance from the wealthy nations.

With the war on terrorism absorbing increased government spending and the economy in recession, it might seem an inopportune time to talk about additional government expenditures. But this is a time when people are willing to think outside their individual needs and concerns and when they are painfully aware that the wellbeing of all the world's people is of direct importance to the United States. The humanitarian and economic reasons to take action against global infectious disease have never been more compelling.

Chapter 2

Will Globalization Harm Developing Nations?

Chapter Preface

The term *globalization* encompasses the idea that the world is becoming increasingly connected—both economically and culturally. Thomas Friedman, author of *The Lexus and the Olive Tree: Understanding Globalization*, describes globalization as "the integration of everything with everything else . . . Globalization is the integration of markets, finance, and technology in a way that shrinks the world from a size medium to a size small."

It seems like a simple idea, but globalization is a highly complex—and much contested—concept. Researchers argue about its definition, whether it is occurring or not, and whether it primarily affects economies or cultures. At the heart of many of these debates is whether globalization benefits or harms developing nations.

Critics of globalization argue that it exploits and oppresses the poor in developing nations. Of key concern is the role of transnational corporations (known as TNCs) and their role in foreign investment and business arrangements in which items are manufactured in developing nations and exported to developed nations. "More than any other single institution, it is the transnational corporation which has come to be regarded as the primary shaper of the contemporary global economy," says Peter Dicken, author of *Global Shift: Transforming the World Economy*. TNCs can often produce goods more cheaply in the developing world than they can in wealthier nations. TNCs contribute to the economies of developing countries—but critics charge that TNCs exploit workers by paying them little to work long hours in substandard conditions.

Defenders of globalization argue that while the operations of TNCs may seem exploitative, developing nations do benefit from the economic growth TNCs provide. In this view, developing nations' acceptance of TNCs—and their sometimes questionable labor practices—is a necessary step toward participation in the global economy. Scholar Richard Wright maintains that such participation and the economic growth that comes with it benefits even the poorest workers: "Tracking nations with the most open, most globalized economies over the last several decades, [World Bank economists David Dollar and Aart Kraay] found that, as national income grew, the fraction of the economic pie going to the bottom fifth of the income scale didn't shrink. The rising tide indeed seemed to lift all boats."

The controversy over TNCs is just one part of a larger debate about whether the process of globalization is resulting in the exploitation and domination of poorer nations by richer ones—a phenomenon many refer to as "the West over the rest." In the following chapter, authors further explore the economic and cultural aspects of this debate.

Globalization Harms Developing Nations' Economies

by Dani Rodrik

About the author: *Dani Rodrik is a professor of international political economy at the John F. Kennedy School of Government at Harvard University.*

Advocates of global economic integration hold out utopian visions of the prosperity that developing countries will reap if they open their borders to commerce and capital. This hollow promise diverts poor nations' attention and resources from the key domestic innovations needed to spur economic growth.

A senior U.S. Treasury official recently urged Mexico's government to work harder to reduce violent crime because "such high levels of crime and violence may drive away foreign investors." This admonition nicely illustrates how foreign trade and investment have become the ultimate yardstick for evaluating the social and economic policies of governments in developing countries. Forget the slum dwellers or campesinos who live amidst crime and poverty throughout the developing world. Just mention "investor sentiment" or "competitiveness in world markets" and policymakers will come to attention in a hurry.

Underlying this perversion of priorities is a remarkable consensus on the imperative of global economic integration. Openness to trade and investment flows is no longer viewed simply as a component of a country's development strategy; it has mutated into the most potent catalyst for economic growth known to humanity. Predictably, senior officials of the World Trade Organization (WTO), International Monetary Fund (IMF), and other international financial agencies incessantly repeat the openness mantra. In recent years, however, faith in integration has spread quickly to political leaders and policymakers around the world.

Joining the world economy is no longer a matter simply of dismantling barriers to trade and investment. Countries now must also comply with a long list of admission requirements, from new patent rules to more rigorous banking standards. The apostles of economic integration prescribe comprehensive institutional reforms that took today's advanced countries generations to accomplish, so that developing countries can, as the cliché goes, maximize the gains and minimize the risks of participation in the world economy. Global integration has become, for all practical purposes, a substitute for a development strategy.

This trend is bad news for the world's poor. The new agenda of global integration rests on shaky empirical ground and seriously distorts policymakers' priorities. By focusing on international integration, governments in poor nations divert human resources, administrative capabilities, and political capital away from more urgent development priorities such as education, public health, industrial capacity, and social cohesion. This emphasis also undermines nascent democratic institutions by removing the choice of development strategy from public debate.

> *"Joining the world economy is no longer a matter simply of dismantling barriers to trade and investment. Countries now must also comply with a long list of admission requirements."*

World markets are a source of technology and capital; it would be silly for the developing world not to exploit these opportunities. But globalization is not a shortcut to development. Successful economic growth strategies have always required a judicious blend of imported practices with domestic institutional innovations. Policymakers need to forge a domestic growth strategy by relying on domestic investors and domestic institutions. The costliest downside of the integrationist faith is that it crowds out serious thinking and efforts along such lines.

Excuses, Excuses

Countries that have bought wholeheartedly into the integration orthodoxy are discovering that openness does not deliver on its promise. Despite sharply lowering their barriers to trade and investment since the 1980s, scores of countries in Latin America and Africa are stagnating or growing less rapidly than in the heyday of import substitution during the 1960s and 1970s. By contrast, the fastest growing countries are China, India, and others in East and Southeast Asia. Policymakers in these countries have also espoused trade and investment liberalization, but they have done so in an unorthodox manner—gradually, sequentially, and only after an initial period of high growth—and as part of a broader policy package with many unconventional features.

The disappointing outcomes with deep liberalization have been absorbed into the faith with remarkable aplomb. Those who view global integration as the prerequisite for economic development now simply add the caveat that opening borders is insufficient. Reaping the gains from openness, they argue, also requires a full complement of institutional reforms.

Consider trade liberalization. Asking any World Bank economist what a successful trade-liberalization program requires will likely elicit a laundry list of measures beyond the simple reduction of tariff and nontariff barriers: tax reform to make up for lost tariff revenues; social safety nets to compensate displaced workers; administrative reform to bring trade practices into compliance with WTO rules; labor market reform to enhance worker mobility across industries; technological assistance to upgrade firms hurt by import competition; and training programs to ensure that export-oriented firms and investors have access to skilled workers. As the promise of trade liberalization fails to materialize, the prerequisites keep expanding. For example, Clare Short, Great Britain's secretary of state for international development, recently added universal provision of health and education to the list.

In the financial arena, integrationists have pushed complementary reforms with even greater fanfare and urgency. The prevailing view in Washington and other Group of Seven (G-7) capitals is that weaknesses in banking systems, prudential regulation, and corporate governance were at the heart of the Asian financial crisis of the late 1990s. Hence the ambitious efforts by the G-7 to establish international codes and standards covering fiscal transparency, monetary and financial policy, banking supervision, data dissemination, corporate governance, and accounting standards. The Financial Stability Forum (FSF)—a G-7 organization with minimal representation from developing nations—has designated 12 of these standards as essential for creating sound financial systems in developing countries. The full FSF compendium includes an additional 59 standards the agency considers "relevant for sound financial systems," bringing the total number of codes to 71. To fend off speculative capital movements, the IMF and the G-7 also typically urge developing countries to accumulate foreign reserves and avoid exchange-rate regimes that differ from a "hard peg" (tying the value of one's currency to that of a more stable currency, such as the U.S. dollar) or a "pure float" (letting the market determine the appropriate exchange rate).

A cynic might wonder whether the point of all these prerequisites is merely to provide easy cover for eventual failure. Integrationists can conveniently blame disappointing growth performance or a financial crisis on "slippage" in the implementation of complementary reforms rather than on a poorly designed liberalization. So if Bangladesh's freer trade policy does not produce a large enough spurt in growth, the World Bank concludes that the problem must involve lagging reforms in public administration or continued "political uncertainty" (always a favorite). And if Argentina gets caught up in a confidence crisis despite significant trade and financial liberalization, the IMF reasons that structural reforms have been inadequate and must be deepened.

Free Trade-Offs

Most (but certainly not all) of the institutional reforms on the integrationist agenda are perfectly sensible, and in a world without financial, administrative, or political constraints, there would be little argument about the need to adopt them. But in the real world, governments face difficult choices over how to deploy their fiscal resources, administrative capabilities, and political capital. Setting institutional priorities to maximize integration into the global economy has real opportunity costs.

Consider some illustrative trade-offs. World Bank trade economist Michael Finger has estimated that a typical developing country must spend $150 million to implement requirements under just three WTO agreements (those on customs valuation, sanitary and phytosanitary measures, and trade-related intellectual property rights). As Finger notes, this sum equals a year's development budget for many least-developed countries. And while the budgetary burden of implementing financial codes and standards has never been fully estimated, it undoubtedly entails a substantial diversion of fiscal and human resources as well. Should governments in developing countries train more bank auditors and accountants, even if those investments mean fewer secondary-school teachers or reduced spending on primary education for girls?

In the area of legal reform, should governments focus their energies on "importing" legal codes and standards or on improving existing domestic legal institutions? In Turkey, a weak coalition government spent several months during 1999 gathering political support for a bill providing foreign investors the protection of international arbitration. But wouldn't a better long-run strategy have involved reforming the existing legal regime for the benefit of foreign and domestic investors alike?

In public health, should governments promote the reverse engineering of patented basic medicines and the importation of low-cost generic drugs from "unauthorized" suppliers, even if doing so means violating WTO rules against such practices? When South Africa passed legislation in 1997 allowing imports of patented AIDS drugs from cheaper sources, the country came under severe pressure from Western governments, which argued that the South African policy conflicted with WTO rules on intellectual property.

> *"Despite sharply lowering their barriers to trade and investment since the 1980s, scores of countries in Latin America and Africa are stagnating or growing less rapidly."*

How much should politicians spend on social protection policies in view of the fiscal constraints imposed by market "discipline"? Peru's central bank holds foreign reserves equal to 15 months of imports as an insurance policy against the sudden capital outflows that financially open economies often experience. The opportunity cost of this policy amounts to almost 1 percent of gross domestic product annually—more than enough to fund a generous antipoverty program.

How should governments choose their exchange-rate regimes? During the last four decades, virtually every growth boom in the developing world has been accompanied by a controlled depreciation of the domestic currency. Yet financial openness makes it all but impossible to manage the exchange rate.

How should policymakers focus their anticorruption strategies? Should they target the high-level corruption that foreign investors often decry or the petty corruption that affects the poor the most? Perhaps, as the proponents of permanent normal trade relations with China argued in the recent U.S. debate, a government that is forced to protect the rights of foreign investors will become more inclined to protect the rights of its own citizens as well. But this is, at best, a trickledown strategy of institutional reform. Shouldn't reforms target the desired ends directly—whether those ends are the rule of law, improved observance of human rights, or reduced corruption?

> *"A strategy of 'globalization above all' crowds out alternatives that are potentially more development-friendly."*

The rules for admission into the world economy not only reflect little awareness of development priorities, they are often completely unrelated to sensible economic principles. For instance, WTO agreements on anti-dumping, subsidies and countervailing measures, agriculture, textiles, and trade-related intellectual property rights lack any economic rationale beyond the mercantilist interests of a narrow set of powerful groups in advanced industrial countries. Bilateral and regional trade agreements are typically far worse, as they impose even tighter prerequisites on developing countries in return for crumbs of enhanced "market access." For example, the African Growth and Opportunity Act signed by U.S. President Clinton in May 2000 provides increased access to the U.S. market only if African apparel manufacturers use U.S.-produced fabric and yarns. This restriction severely limits the potential economic spillovers in African countries.

There are similar questions about the appropriateness of financial codes and standards. These codes rely heavily on an Anglo-American style of corporate governance and an arm's-length model of financial development. They close off alternative paths to financial development of the sort that have been followed by many of today's rich countries (for example, Germany, Japan, or South Korea).

In each of these areas, a strategy of "globalization above all" crowds out alternatives that are potentially more development-friendly. Many of the institutional reforms needed for insertion into the world economy can be independently desirable or produce broader economic benefits. But these priorities do not necessarily coincide with the priorities of a comprehensive development agenda.

Asian Myths

Even if the institutional reforms needed to join the international economic community are expensive and preclude investments in other crucial areas, pro-globalization advocates argue that the vast increases in economic growth that invariably result from insertion into the global marketplace will more than compensate for those costs. Take the East Asian tigers or China, the advocates say. Where would they be without international trade and foreign capital flows?

That these countries reaped enormous benefits from their progressive integration into the world economy is undeniable. But look closely at what policies produced those results, and you will find little that resembles today's rule book.

Countries like South Korea and Taiwan had to abide by few international constraints and pay few of the modern costs of integration during their formative growth experience in the 1960s and 1970s. At that time, global trade rules were sparse and economies faced almost none of today's common pressures to open their borders to capital flows. So these countries combined their outward orientation with unorthodox policies: high levels of tariff and nontariff barriers, public ownership of large segments of banking and industry, export subsidies, domestic-content requirements, patent and copyright infringements, and restrictions on capital flows (including on foreign direct investment). Such policies are either precluded by today's trade rules or are highly frowned upon by organizations like the IMF and the World Bank.

China also followed a highly unorthodox two-track strategy, violating practically every rule in the guidebook (including, most notably, the requirement of private property rights). India, which significantly raised its economic growth rate in the early 1980s, remains one of the world's most highly protected economies.

All of these countries liberalized trade gradually, over a period of decades, not years. Significant import liberalization did not occur until after a transition to high economic growth had taken place. And far from wiping the institutional slate clean, all of these nations managed to eke growth out of their existing institutions, imperfect as they may have been. Indeed, when some of the more successful Asian economies gave in to Western pressure to liberalize capital flows rapidly, they were rewarded with the Asian financial crisis.

That is why these countries can hardly be considered poster children for today's global rules. South Korea, China, India, and the other Asian success cases had the freedom to do their own thing, and they used that freedom abundantly. Today's globalizers would be unable to replicate these experiences without running afoul of the IMF or the WTO.

The Asian experience highlights a deeper point: A sound overall development strategy that produces high economic growth is far more effective in achieving integration with the world economy than a purely integrationist strategy that relies on openness to work its magic. In other words, the globalizers have it exactly backwards. Integration is the result, not the cause, of economic and social development. A relatively protected economy like Vietnam is integrating with the world economy much more rapidly than an open economy like Haiti because Vietnam, unlike Haiti, has a reasonably functional economy and polity.

Integration into the global economy, unlike tariff rates or capital-account regulations, is not something that policymakers control directly. Telling finance ministers in developing nations that they should increase their "participation in world trade" is as meaningful as telling them that they need to improve technological capabilities—and just as helpful. Policymakers need to know which strategies will produce these results, and whether the specific prescriptions that the current orthodoxy offers are up to the task.

Too Good to Be True

Do lower trade barriers spur greater economic progress? The available studies reveal no systematic relationship between a country's average level of tariff and nontariff barriers and its subsequent economic growth rate. If anything, the evidence for the 1990s indicates a positive relationship between import tariffs and economic growth. The only clear pattern is that countries dismantle their trade restrictions as they grow richer. This finding explains why today's rich countries, with few exceptions, embarked on modern economic growth behind protective barriers but now display low trade barriers.

The absence of a strong negative relationship between trade restrictions and economic growth may seem surprising in view of the ubiquitous claim that trade liberalization promotes higher growth. Indeed, the economics literature is replete with cross-national studies concluding that growth and economic dynamism are strongly linked to more open trade policies. A particularly influential study finds that economies that are "open," by the study's own definition, grew 2.45 percentage points faster annually than closed ones—an enormous difference.

Upon closer look, however, such studies turn out to be unreliable. In a detailed review of the empirical literature, University of Maryland economist Francisco Rodriguez and I have found a major gap between the results that economists have actually obtained and the policy conclusions they have typically drawn. For example, in many cases economists blame poor growth on the government's failure to liberalize trade policies, when the true culprits are ineffective institutions, geographic determinants (such as location in a tropical region), or inappropriate macroeconomic policies (such as an overvalued exchange rate). Once these misdiagnoses are corrected, any meaningful relationship across countries between the level of trade barriers and economic growth evaporates.

> *"Telling . . . developing nations that they should increase their 'participation in world trade' is as meaningful as telling them that they need to improve technological capabilities."*

The evidence on the benefits of liberalizing capital flows is even weaker. In theory, the appeal of capital mobility seems obvious: If capital is free to enter (and leave) markets based on the potential return on investment, the result will be an efficient allocation of global resources. But in reality, financial markets are inherently unstable, subject to bubbles (rational or otherwise), panics, short-sightedness, and self-fulfilling prophecies. There is plenty of evidence that financial liberalization is often followed by financial crash—just ask Mexico, Thailand, or Turkey—while there is little convincing evidence to suggest that higher rates of economic growth follow capital-account liberalization.

Perhaps the most disingenuous argument in favor of liberalizing international financial flows is that the threat of massive and sudden capital movements serves to discipline policymakers in developing nations who might otherwise manage their economies irresponsibly. In other words, governments might be less inclined to squander their societies' resources if such actions would spook foreign lenders. In practice, however, the discipline argument falls apart. Behavior in international capital markets is dominated by mood swings unrelated to fundamentals. In good times, a government with a chronic fiscal deficit has an easier time financing its spending when it can borrow funds from investors abroad; witness Russia prior to 1998 or Argentina in the 1990s. And in bad times, governments may be forced to adopt inappropriate policies in order to conform to the biases of foreign investors; witness the excessively restrictive monetary and fiscal policies in much of East Asia in the immediate aftermath of the Asian financial crisis. A key reason why Malaysia was able to recover so quickly after the imposition of capital controls in September 1998 was that Prime Minister Mahathir Mohamad resisted the high interest rates and tight fiscal policies that South Korea, Thailand, and Indonesia adopted at the behest of the International Monetary Fund.

Growth Begins at Home

Well-trained economists are justifiably proud of the textbook case in favor of free trade. For all the theory's simplicity, it is one of our profession's most significant achievements. However, in their zeal to promote the virtues of trade, the most ardent proponents are peddling a cartoon version of the argument, vastly overstating the effectiveness of economic openness as a tool for fostering development. Such claims only endanger broad public acceptance of the real article because they unleash unrealistic expectations about the benefits of free trade. Neither economic theory nor empirical evidence guarantees that deep trade liberalization will deliver higher economic growth. Economic openness and all its accouterments do not deserve the priority they typically receive in the development strategies pushed by leading multilateral organizations.

Countries that have achieved long-term economic growth have usually combined the opportunities offered by world markets with a growth strategy that mobilizes the capabilities of domestic institutions and investors. Designing such a growth strategy is both harder and easier than implementing typical integration policies. It is harder because the binding constraints on growth are usually country specific and do not respond well to standardized recipes. But it is easier because once those constraints are targeted, relatively simple policy changes

63

can yield enormous economic payoffs and start a virtuous cycle of growth and additional reform.

Unorthodox innovations that depart from the integration rule book are typically part and parcel of such strategies. Public enterprises during the Meiji restoration in Japan; township and village enterprises in China; an export processing zone in Mauritius; generous tax incentives for priority investments in Taiwan; extensive credit subsidies in South Korea; infant-industry protection in Brazil during the 1960s and 1970s—these are some of the innovations that have been instrumental in kick-starting investment and growth in the past. None came out of a Washington economist's tool kit.

Few of these experiments have worked as well when transplanted to other settings, only underscoring the decisive importance of local conditions. To be effective, development strategies need to be tailored to prevailing domestic institutional strengths. There is simply no alternative to a homegrown business plan. Policymakers who look to Washington and financial markets for the answers are condemning themselves to mimicking the conventional wisdom du jour, and to eventual disillusionment.

Globalization Harms Developing Nations' Cultures

by J. Scott Tynes

About the author: *J. Scott Tynes is a staff writer for the* Star, *a weekly newspaper of politics, economics, and culture, published in English in the nation of Jordan.*

Part I: Understanding Globalization and Cultural Imperialism

The concept of globalization and the new religion of the masses, capitalism, needs to come under even greater scrutiny. The developed world beats a drum of such deafening proportion, the cries and needs of smaller niche participants are being drowned out.

At present the idea and implementation of "globalization" is largely Western in its scope. It remains a Westernizing process integrally tied to the ideals of capitalism, serving to broaden the gap Western nations have enjoyed economically, politically and militarily.

It is the inherent interest of globalization to bring forward values and ideals largely Western in nature because they are understood and thereby seen as superior. They provide a sense of control, a sense of the known. This is not to suggest these ideals are necessarily in direct opposition to any Eastern or Occidental economic design. But it does posit an idea no less disturbing. These ideals are so readily available, so pervasive, they have begun to supercede the native values of developing nations.

Imperialism in the old world sense was an economic, political or military method used to undermine the sovereignty of a nation. The new imperialism is a cultural imperialism, using the machinery of the rapidly expanding communications network to inundate nations with Western ideology.

To suggest "imperialism" is to suggest a deliberate attempt by Western capitalist countries to dominate the mass media of other nations and affect the ways they think and live their lives. How deliberate an attempt is being made is not clear. But the advantages of such domination are easily identifiable. The creation of markets for Western products and the opening of labor markets with workers eager to earn money soon put right back into the system is of primary importance.

Western economies entered a period of change from labor to service and information economies over the last half-century. As such the maintenance and development of information pathways and communications technologies has become vital to economic growth. A need for control and domination of world communication and data flows has emerged. Having

> *"[Western] ideals are so readily available, so pervasive, they have begun to supercede the native values of developing nations."*

this control ensures continued economic expansion and the continual growth now referred to as globalization.

It is not too far a stretch to see how old imperialist desires can evolve and integrate into capitalist interests to control a variety of communication and data flow technologies, the laws that govern them and even the bandwidth that they occupy.

The emergence of transnational corporations (TNCs) was the clarion burst announcing the arrival of a new way of handling global business. Business would no longer be limited by geographic boundaries. Every corner of the earth could become a potential market; every corner could provide labor, so long as control over key aspects of the development could be maintained. Such control allows for a directed diversification, the "globalization" of production and advertising.

This change is bringing about a gradual erosion of the sovereignty of many nations. Overseeing bodies such as the World Bank and the International Monetary Fund (IMF) were brought in to monitor and control this development and shape it to fit Western standards of success and growth; sometimes at great disadvantage to their protégés.

A study by the Canadian Department of Communications revealed "the information revolution may accelerate the erosion of national sovereignty by further increasing the dominance of multi-national corporations in the world economy."

Globalization leaves developing nations as niche participants, requiring them to find some part of the production process they can perform better or cheaper than any other nation. It forces them to do that exclusively, often ignoring the importance of internal needs so they can remain a part of the global marketplace.

Western Control of Communications and Data Flows

Real concerns begin to emerge when direct connections suggesting any "imperialist" attitudes are examined. Currently there are five areas of control, which all bring forth a rather ominous conclusion. Efforts to control communications and data flows suggest, whether deliberately planned or not, globalization is resulting in, at the very least, a cultural imperialism.

The majority of information transmitted between nations is that of transnational corporations (TNCs), coordinating and maintaining control over various branches of their organization. The data they are relaying involves information directly affecting a nation's economy: Raw material supplies, inventory, pricing, labor policy, tax matters, currency holdings and investment plans. These are vital national interests. TNCs end up making decisions affecting these nations from distant locales all the while maintaining their own priorities, totally without the oversight of the national authority.

Remote sensing, where orbiting satellites are capable of mapping out terrain to reveal hidden resources and potential physical trouble spots, is currently employed by military and corporate interests to maintain global dominance and dependency. Resources such as agricultural and oceanic phenomena revealed with this technology can greatly aid developing nations. It could enable them to greatly accelerate their development, taking advantage of exclusive data instead of wasting resources on dead ends.

Database construction and access is controlled, again, for corporate and military gain. The majority of databases in existence are for the purpose of maintaining and supporting the needs of TNCs. These databases contain customer names, payroll information, property ownership, credit rating, and health information. This is vital in-

> *"Whether deliberately planned or not, globalization is resulting in . . . a cultural imperialism."*

formation key to interests in globalist expansion. Understanding and controlling this information provides an upper hand in the control of markets and the focus of advertising.

Direct Broadcast Satellites (DBS), seen on the sides of most every home, provide just what they advertise: Direct access with little or no interference from a national authority. Images and programming are beamed directly circumventing any control or supervision, any national interest. Despite the international community's cries for prior consent to programming before broadcast, the US has replied that such consent restricts the "free flow of information" and as such violates the US right to free speech.

Western governments even extend control over slots in space for satellites to orbit. This allows TNCs primary, nearly exclusive, access to markets, allowing for more rapidly developed communication amongst the various global branches of these corporations. Nations shut out of the skies are not only limited by restricted access but also subjugated by the data these satellites communicate.

This control creates markets for products by exportation of commercials and the portrayal of the "good life" as seen through Western television programs and films. Once the desire is created within these new markets, a "globalization" door opens for potential labor markets. Once people want products they have seen, once they feel they "need" these products to be happy, they are willing to work to satisfy their desire.

Advertising and the development of a globalized structure such as unified currencies can bode ill for developing countries if they operate unaware. Western advertising currently helps to maintain monopolies, it forms and guides tastes, and shifts consumer demand to largely Western interests. Western control can come through

> *"Western ideals can be more 'enlightened,' but they are not necessarily so and certainly not superior by their nature."*

these less direct means or through financial controls handed down from overseeing bodies. Regardless of how it arrives, the effect is to put the control of a nation's economy and the culture of its people in the hands of those whose only real interest is profit.

Part II: The "Free" Flow of Information

Concern is growing over US government protection of its abilities to reach untapped markets with targeted advertising under claims of "free information flows."

The World Press Freedom Committee (WPFC) seemed to concur that such actions were legitimate saying, "We believe that the free flow of information is essential for mutual understanding and world peace." The WPFC sees a correlation between advertising and freedom of the press, suggesting without the income generated through advertising a free press could not exist. Thus suggesting without the advertising of large transnational corporations (TNCs) a free press cannot exist and therefore those who resist this free flow of advertising/information are resisting the free press and thereby resisting freedom.

When globalization is examined in the light of the five previously discussed more passive efforts, some degree of cultural imperialism can be divined. But a more active form exists in activities such as this, termed "soft power." Soft power strategies are designed to control specific information causing people of other resistant nations to act and think as the provider of this information. By infiltrating a nation through communication pathways a controlling nation can defeat resistance to globalization desires from the inside.

From a political perspective, using propaganda to stabilize ethnic unrest and promote democracy is a positive thing, but it also gives birth to a cultural development for the acceptance of capitalism; something perhaps not desired by those being stabilized and developed—at the very least this development may not be in their best interests.

Soft power proves to be cultural imperialism with a twist. Soft power, unlike the previous five methodologies, is a blatant attempt at control. Such attempts often yield results opposite of those desired. Soft power is cultural imperialism naked and unabashed. As such it rarely works.

Any effects, whether active as in the case of soft power, or a more passive means such as control over communication and data flows, are in the end filtered by the cultural capacity of the receiver. The bias of both the generator of such a message and the bias of the receiver must be considered.

But the bias of an individual is really too vague to completely explain the resistance or lack of resistance a particular nation has to cultural attacks. The most lucid explanation of what actually controls a culture's capacity to embrace or reject outside input is found in an examination of the number and complexity of the culture's organizations and institutions.

In instances where these mediators "places of worship, cultural icons, leaders, schools" have a great hold on the culture of the nation through their complexity and history, the input of any imperialist machinery will be rejected outright. When the Shah of Iran made attempts to modernize, and hence Westernize, his nation by filling the airwaves with the glories of the west, his intentions to suppress extremists failed miserably as the people of Iran wholly rejected Western values that so differed from Islamic tradition.

These are traditions and beliefs of such complexity they present formidable resistance to the Western way. This makes the people much less susceptible to "soft power" or other forms of cultural imperialism because a structure is in place. They have an alternative. They are not forced to accept the way of the West as the only means for "salvation."

There are other instances where Western culture is accepted but modified by the receiver. South America has seen instances where on the surface US commercialism is rejected. But digging deeper it is apparent this commercialism/ capitalism/globalism has been taken and modified. American lifestyles seen in film and television are not directly accepted but rather transformed into "Brazilianized faces" and thereby deconstructing and reconstructing a message to more aptly fit a cultural norm.

The Harms of Cultural Imperialism

But at the other extreme are examples where cultural capacities are such that nations sacrifice their own best interest to be part of a globalist system. In Mexico a shift began in the Mexican diet resulting from the penetration of 130 TNCs into the Mexican market. These corporations poured millions of dollars into advertising and promotion for their products and increased the consumption of products that cost twenty times more than comparable native foods.

Yet the foods they promoted were much less nutritious than the native staples. But they made the TNCs money. Their profits increased by close to 27 percent. In essence the Mexican people stopped eating the cheaper and healthier foods of their tradition and their ability and opted for poor, processed, more expensive foodstuffs advertised and promoted by TNCs.

In India many left traditional occupations for more lucrative niche positions allowing them to buy the wares of the west. The television bombarded them with what they "need" and many within India began to accept they actually needed these products. For example, a decade ago India had only three or four brands of soap. Through television advertising and a variety of road shows "a sort of infomercial on wheels" there are now several hundred types of soap; more than nearly any other nation in the world, western or not. India moved from a near dearth of soap to one of the largest consumers in the world through a gradual cultural penetration.

The real need may not exist but the desire created and the acceptance of the advertised can, and many suggest did, change Indian society for the worse. Western ideals can be more "enlightened," but they are not necessarily so and certainly not superior by their nature. When they begin to replace traditional values and ideals that are key to the establishment of a unique sense of cultural identity a very significant danger exists.

Nearly all these unique identities are pared with unique non-Western cultures whose value may not be fully understood by those promoting such development. And most recently many of these cultures have been Islamic prompting fears of the wars of "us" versus "them." The "free" flow of information's real cost might be in the homogenization of global cultures and in the end the loss of a diversity key to the development of man.

Part III: Cultural Imperalism: Do All the Pieces Fit?

It should be more and more apparent a degree of cultural imperialism is inherent in the structure of globalization and capitalism. But by its very nature it is more and more difficult to identify any fingerprints that would point to a specific organizer of any effort to implant capitalism in the third and rapidly shrinking second world.

The reality is the US government is not capable of organizing and implementing a cultural imperialist policy. One hand rarely knows what the other is doing in the US government. To suggest an organized effort by the US to be cultural imperialists is ludicrous in light of its difficulties in implementing economic policies at home.

> *"What we are witnessing now is . . . an imperialism that has the markings of transnational corporate cultural domination."*

But US and other Western governments are participants and enablers through the economic relationships they have with transnational corporations (TNCs). What we are witnessing now is not governmental domination, not a governmental imperialism like the imperialism of old, but instead an imperialism that has the markings of transnational corporate cultural domination, albeit American/Western in nature.

Again, though, to suggest the TNCs of the world have organized and focused on a cultural imperialist agenda and are utilizing their influence over the nations of the world to this end is a bit premature, ringing a bit of conspiracy theories of *Illuminati* and the like that have recently made the rounds in movie theaters.

TNCs presently have a largely free reign across the globe and do have a motive to expose and exploit the markets available to them. But TNCs do not operate from an organized cultural imperialist position. They simply cannot. To do so would be to operate in a vacuum away from the critical eyes of the rest of the world. But it is also not in their best interest to do so.

> *"Cultural imperialism is perhaps best defined as capitalism's attempts at domination."*

TNC motives are pure and simple: profit and markets. When those motives coincide with that of another TNC, the result may be a 'cultural imperialist action.' For example, if two corporations see that combining forces and influencing the government of a developing nation might work to their mutual benefit, they will do so. TNCs usually do not operate in this spirit. They compete with one another. Sharing profits is not part of their capitalist makeup.

Cultural imperialism exists; but when the curtain is raised, and it is examined in detail, it is a perhaps less sensational form than initially imagined. There exists little real organization and focus in creating these imperialist intrusions other than simple profit motives.

TNCs are interested in the bottom line and Western nations are dependent on the success of TNCs to grease the gears that keep their nation afloat. This has become the nature of the modern nation state. Economic power has replaced military power as the most important, most wieldy, form of control and expansion. Countries are less interested in capturing new geographic territory, and more interested in economic dominance that in the end builds their own coffers. Successful economies mean a country can survive and thrive.

It is a complex interrelation that results in legislation and actions that would sometimes seem to point to coordinated efforts at capitalist global domination. TNC advisors to nations on UN councils controlling satellite positioning make many very nervous.

There has begun a great deal of speculation and fear about a unified globe. The idea of a single currency such as the euro and singular bodies to control information flows and economic agendas makes many, quite justly, anxious.

It should be clear that removing impediments to economic expansion benefits the large before the small. Opening the doors of small and developing nations means TNCs can waltz in with their tremendous resources and dominate the economy. It is a scary and very real thought.

No Single Culprit

But rather than finding a singular organized culprit for cultural domination such as TNCs or Western governments responsible, it is more likely the villain is capitalism itself. It is the true motivator of all those involved. It would perhaps serve the agendas of many afraid of a conspiracy to raise a curtain and find a single group to point a finger at. Some have seen the G8 [Canada, France, Germany, Italy, Japan, Russia, the United Kingdom, and the United States] or WTO [World Trade Organization] as the wizards running the show. But the implementation and organization at this point does not suggest this. The pieces are there, but they have yet to be fully assembled.

Some consideration of the cultural capacities of the nations involved is also a point of note. Cultural imperialism will not always be completely successful. Its results may vary from complete failure in nations with complex organizations and institutions to adaptations of capitalism in nations that are less complex and organized. It might also result in the complete abandonment of those institutions and organizations in nations desperate to have the 'good life' of the West.

The import of Western advertising and programming into the former communist nation of Albania and the introduction of a prime piece of Western capitalism, the pyramid scheme, led to the destruction of that nation. Albanians living for years beside Western nations saw the 'good life' transmitted across the border to them. As they lived their lives under the oppression of communism desires grew, fed by the advertising and programming of western television and radio. When given the chance to have it all, albeit through risky pyramid schemes, they risked it all. Unfortunately they lost. But no single figure or group can be blamed.

Cultural imperialism is perhaps best defined as capitalism's attempts at domination. Capitalism has become the new opiate of many, many people. But it must be recognized that capitalism is an autonomous entity, part of Western society but not specifically controlled by any single party or organized group.

It exists because people want—they want newer, they want better and they want more. Those that are able to control their wants, or those whose wants don't fit the mainstream mold are able to sidestep the impact.

As long as a 'want' exists on a global level, capitalism and its brother, globalization, will have at its core methods of transmission resulting in cultural imperialism. Advertising from Western TNCs will continue to inundate the globe, databases will continue to be used primarily for TNC benefit, satellite positioning and the information they provide will remain in the hands of the already powerful, and old men in grass huts will continue to watch reruns of *I Love Lucy* as they drift off into capitalist dreams of the good life, wearing Levi's, drinking Coke and driving a brand new Mercedes Benz.

Globalization Benefits Developing Nations' Economies

by the *Economist*

About the author: *The* Economist *is a weekly magazine of business and politics.*

For the most part, it seems, workers in rich countries have little to fear from globalisation, and a lot to gain. But is the same thing true for workers in poor countries? The answer is that they are even more likely than their rich-country counterparts to benefit, because they have less to lose and more to gain.

Orthodox economics takes an optimistic line on integration and the developing countries. Openness to foreign trade and investment should encourage capital to flow to poor economies. In the developing world, capital is scarce, so the returns on investment there should be higher than in the industrialised countries, where the best opportunities to make money by adding capital to labour have already been used up. If poor countries lower their barriers to trade and investment, the theory goes, rich foreigners will want to send over some of their capital.

If this inflow of resources arrives in the form of loans or portfolio investment, it will supplement domestic savings and loosen the financial constraint on additional investment by local companies. If it arrives in the form of new foreign-controlled [investments], FDI, so much the better: this kind of capital brings technology and skills from abroad packaged along with it, with less financial risk as well. In either case, the addition to investment ought to push incomes up, partly by raising the demand for labour and partly by making labour more productive.

This is why workers in FDI-receiving countries should be in an even better position to profit from integration than workers in FDI-sending countries. Also, with or without inflows of foreign capital, the same static and dynamic gains from trade should apply in developing countries as in rich ones. This gains-from-trade logic often arouses suspicion, because the benefits seem to come from nowhere. Surely one side or the other must lose. Not so. The benefits that a rich country gets through trade do not come at the expense of its poor-country trading partners, or vice versa. Recall that according to the theory, trade is a positive-sum game. In all these transactions, both sides—exporters and importers, borrowers and lenders, shareholders and workers—can gain.

What, if anything, might spoil the simple theory and make things go awry? Plenty, say the sceptics.

First, they argue, telling developing countries to grow through trade, rather than through building industries to serve domestic markets, involves a fallacy of composition. If all poor countries tried to do this simultaneously, the price of their exports would be driven down on world markets. The success of the East Asian tigers [nations in Southeast Asia that performed well economically in the 1900s], the argument continues, owed much to the fact that so many other developing countries chose to discourage trade

> *"If poor countries lower their barriers to trade and investment, . . . rich foreigners will want to send over some of their capital."*

rather than promote it. This theory of "export pessimism" was influential with many developing-country governments up until the 1980s, and seems to lie behind the thinking of many sceptics today.

A second objection to the openness-is-good orthodoxy concerns not trade but FDI. The standard thinking assumes that foreign capital pays for investment that makes economic sense—the kind that will foster development. Experience shows that this is often not so. For one reason or another, the inflow of capital may produce little or nothing of value, sometimes less than nothing. The money may be wasted or stolen. If it was borrowed, all there will be to show for it is an insupportable debt to foreigners. Far from merely failing to advance development, this kind of financial integration sets it back.

Third, the sceptics point out, workers in developing countries lack the rights, legal protections and union representation enjoyed by their counterparts in rich countries. This is why, in the eyes of the multinationals, hiring them makes such good sense. Lacking in bargaining power, workers do not benefit as they should from an increase in the demand for labour. Their wages do not go up. They may have no choice but to work in sweatshops, suffering unhealthy or dangerous conditions, excessive hours or even physical abuse. In the worst cases, children as well as adults are the victims.

Is Trade Good for Growth?

All this seems very complicated. Can the doubters be answered simply by measuring the overall effect of openness on economic growth? Some economists think so, and have produced a variety of much-quoted econometric studies apparently confirming that trade promotes development. Studies by Jeffrey Sachs and Andrew Warner at Harvard, by David Dollar and Aart Kraay of the World Bank, and by Jeffrey Frankel of Harvard and David Romer of Berkeley, are among the most frequently cited. Studies such as these are enough to convince most economists that trade does indeed promote growth. But they cannot be said to settle the matter. If the application of econometrics to other big, complicated questions in economics is any guide, they probably never will: the precise economic linkages that underlie the correlations may always be too difficult to uncover.

This is why a good number of economists, including some of the most distinguished advocates of liberal trade, are unpersuaded by this kind of work. For every regression "proving" that trade promotes growth, it is too easy to tweak a choice of variable here and a period of analysis there to "prove" that it does not. Among the sceptics, Dani Rodrik has led the assault on the pro-trade regression studies. But economists such as Jagdish Bhagwati and T.N. Srinivasan, both celebrated advocates of trade liberalisation, are also pretty scathing about the regression evidence.

Look elsewhere, though, and there is no lack of additional evidence, albeit of a more variegated and less easily summarised sort, that trade promotes development. Of the three criticisms just stated of the orthodox preference for liberal trade, the first and most influential down the years has been the "export pessimism" argument—the idea that liberalising trade will be self-defeating if too many developing countries try to do it simultaneously. What does the evidence say about that?

Pessimism Confounded

It does not say that the claim is nonsense. History shows that the prediction of persistently falling export prices has proved correct for some commodity exporters: demand for some commodities has failed to keep pace with growth in global incomes. And nobody will ever know what would have happened over the past few decades if all the developing countries had promoted trade more vigorously, because they didn't. But there are good practical reasons to regard the pessimism argument, as applied to poor-country exports in general, as wrong.

The developing countries as a group may be enormous in terms of geography and population, but in economic terms they are small. Taken together, the exports of all the world's poor and middle-income countries (including comparative giants such as China, India, Brazil and Mexico, big oil exporters such as Saudi Arabia, and large-scale manufacturers such as

"As developing countries grow by exporting, their own demand for imports rises."

South Korea, Taiwan and Malaysia) represent only about 5% of global output. This is an amount roughly equivalent to the gross domestic product (GDP) of Britain. Even if growth in the global demand for imports were somehow capped, a concerted export drive by those parts of the developing world not already engaged in the effort would put no great strain on the global trading system.

In any event, though, the demand for imports is not capped. In effect, export pessimism involves a fallacy of its own—a "lump-of-trade" fallacy, akin to the idea of a "lump of labour" (whereby a growing population is taken to imply an ever-rising rate of unemployment, there being only so many jobs to go around). The overall growth of trade, and the kinds of product that any particular country may buy or sell, are not pre-ordained. As Mr. Bhagwati and Mr. Srinivasan argued in a recent review of the connections between trade and development, forecasts of the poor countries' potential to expand their exports have usually been too low, partly because forecasters concentrate on existing exports and neglect new ones, some of which may be completely unforeseen. Unexpected shifts in the pattern of output have often proved very important.

> *"Almost everywhere, trade has been good for growth."*

Pessimists also make too little of the scope for intra-industry specialisation in trade, which gives developing countries a further set of new opportunities. The same goes for new trade among developing countries, as opposed to trade with the rich world. Often, as developing countries grow, they move away from labour-intensive manufactures to more sophisticated kinds of production: this makes room in the markets they previously served for goods from countries that are not yet so advanced. For example, in the 1970s, Japan withdrew from labour-intensive manufacturing, making way for exports from the East Asian tigers. In the 1980s and 1990s, the tigers did the same, as China began moving into those markets. And as developing countries grow by exporting, their own demand for imports rises.

It is one thing to argue that relying on trade is likely to be self-defeating, as the export pessimists claim; it is another to say that trade actually succeeds in promoting growth. The most persuasive evidence that it does lies in the contrasting experiences from the 1950s onwards of the East Asian tigers, on one side, and the countries that chose to discourage trade and pursue "import-substituting industrialisation" (ISI) on the other, such as India, much of Latin America and much of Africa.

Years ago, in an overlapping series of research projects, great effort went into examining the developing countries' experience with trade policy during the 1950s, 60s and early 70s. This period saw lasting surges of growth without precedent in history. At the outset, South Korea, for instance, was a poor country, with an income per head in 1955 of around $400 (in today's prices), and such poor economic prospects that American officials predicted abject and indefinite dependence on aid. Within a single generation it became a mighty exporter and world-ranking industrial power.

Examining the record up to the 1970s, and the experience of development elsewhere in East Asia and other poor regions of the world, economists at the

Organization for Economic Cooperation and Development (OECD), the World Bank and America's National Bureau of Economic Research came to see the crucial importance of "outward orientation"—that is, of the link between trade and growth. The finding held across a range of countries, regardless of differences in particular policies, institutions and political conditions, all of which varied widely. An unusually impressive body of evidence and analysis discredited the ISI orthodoxy and replaced it with a new one, emphasising trade.

The Trouble with ISI

What was wrong with ISI, according to these researchers? In principle, nothing much; the problems arose over how it worked in practice. The whole idea of ISI was to drive a wedge between world prices and domestic prices, so as to create a bias in favour of producing for the home market and therefore a bias against producing for the export market. In principle, this bias could be modest and uniform; in practice, ISI often produced an anti-export bias both severe and wildly variable between industries. Managing the price-rigging apparatus proved too much for the governments that were attempting it: the policy produced inadvertently large and complex distortions in the pattern of production that often became self-perpetuating and even self-reinforcing. Once investment had been sunk in activities that were profitable only because of tariffs and quotas, any attempt to remove those restrictions was strongly resisted.

ISI also often had an even more pernicious consequence: corruption. The more protected the economy, the greater the gains to be had from illicit activity such as smuggling. The bigger the economic distortions, the bigger the incentive to bribe the government to tweak the rules and tilt the corresponding pattern of surpluses and shortages. Corruption and controls go hand in hand. ISI is not the only instance of this rule in the developing countries, but it has proved especially susceptible to shady practices.

> *"China has embraced the global economy with a vengeance—and see how well it has done."*

Today, developing-country governments are constantly, and rightly, urged to battle corruption and establish the rule of law. This has become a cliché that all sides in the development debate can agree on. But defeating corruption in an economy with pervasive market-suppressing controls, where the rewards to illegality are so high, is extraordinarily hard. This is a connection that people who favour closed or restricted markets prefer to ignore. Limited government, to be sure, is not necessarily clean; but unlimited government, history suggests, never is.

Remember, Remember

On the whole, ISI failed; almost everywhere, trade has been good for growth. The trouble is, this verdict was handed down too long ago. Economists are notoriously ignorant of even recent economic history. The lessons about what world markets did for the tigers in the space of few decades, and the missed opportunities of, say, India (which was well placed to achieve as much), have already been forgotten by many. The East Asian financial crisis of 1997–98 also helped to erase whatever lessons had been learned. And yet the prosperity of East Asia today, crisis and continuing difficulties notwithstanding, bears no comparison with the economic position of India, or Pakistan, or any of the other countries that separated themselves for so much longer from the international economy.

By and large, though, the governments of many developing countries continue to be guided by the open-market orthodoxy that has prevailed since the 1980s. Many want to promote trade in particular and engagement with the world economy in general.

"Some skeptics want, in effect, to punish every export worker in India for the persistence of child labour in parts of the Indian economy."

Even some sceptics might agree that trade is good for growth—but they would add that growth is not necessarily good for poor workers. In fact, it is likely to be bad for the poor, they argue, if the growth in question has been promoted by trade or foreign capital.

Capital inflows, they say, make economies less stable, exposing workers to the risk of financial crisis and to the attentions of western banks and the International Monetary Fund. Also, they argue, growth that is driven by trade or by FDI gives western multinationals a leading role in third-world development. That is bad, because western multinationals are not interested in development at all, only in making bigger profits by ensuring that the poor stay poor. The proof of this, say sceptics, lies in the evidence that economic inequality increases even as developing countries (and rich countries, for that matter) increase their national income, and in the multinationals' direct or indirect use of third-world sweatshops. So if workers' welfare is your main concern, the fact that trade promotes growth, even if true, is beside the point.

Yet there is solid evidence that growth helps the poor. Developing countries that have achieved sustained and rapid growth, as in East Asia, have made remarkable progress in reducing poverty. And the countries where widespread poverty persists, or is worsening, are those where growth is weakest, notably in Africa. Although economic policy can make a big difference to the extent of poverty, in the long run growth is much more important.

It is sometimes claimed that growth is less effective in raising the incomes of the poor in developing countries than in rich countries. This is a fallacy. A recent study confirms that, in 80 countries across the world over the past 40 years, the incomes of the poor have risen one for one with overall growth.

If all this is true, why does global income inequality seem to be widening? First, the evidence is not at all clear-cut. Much depends on how you make your comparisons. An overall comparison of country aggregates—comparing rich countries with poor countries—is generally more encouraging than a comparison of the richest 10% of people in the world with the poorest 10%. In 1975, America's income per head was 19 times bigger than China's ($16,000 against $850); by 1995, the ratio had fallen to six ($23,000 against $3,700). On the other hand it is true that Africa's income per head is rising more slowly than America's: as a result, their income-gap ratio has increased, from 12 in 1975 to 19 in 1995. But it would be odd to blame globalisation for holding Africa back. Africa has been left out of the global economy, partly because its governments used to prefer it that way. China has embraced the global economy with a vengeance—and see how well it has done.

Better than Nothing

Statistical difficulties aside, suppose it were true that global inequality is increasing. Would that be a terrible indictment of globalisation, as sceptics seem to suppose? Perhaps not. It would be disturbing, and extremely surprising, if poor countries engaged in globalisation were failing to catch up—but they aren't, as China and many other avid globalisers show. It would also be disturbing if inequality across the world as a whole were rising because the incomes of the poorest were falling in absolute terms, rather than merely in relative terms—but this is extremely rare. Even in Africa, which is doing so badly in relative terms, incomes have been rising and broader measures of development have been getting better. It may be too little, but it is not nothing, merely because other countries have been doing better.

The sceptics are right to be disturbed by sweatshops, child labour, bonded labour and the other gross abuses that go on in many poor countries (and in the darkest corners of rich ones, too). But what makes people vulnerable to these practices is poverty. It is essential to ask if remedial measures proposed will reduce poverty: otherwise, in attacking the symptoms of the problem, you may be strengthening their underlying cause. It is one thing for the sceptics to insist, for instance, that child labour be prohibited; it is quite another to ensure that the children concerned go to school instead, rather than being driven to scrape a living in even crueller conditions.

"Foreign investors pay their local workers significantly better than other local employers."

The barriers to trade that many sceptics call for seem calculated to make these problems worse. Some sceptics want, in effect, to punish every export worker in India for the persistence of child labour in parts of the Indian economy. This seems morally indefensible as well as counter-productive in economic terms. The same goes for the campaign to hobble the multinationals. The more thoroughly these companies penetrate the markets of the third world, the faster they introduce their capital and working practices, the sooner poverty will retreat and the harder it will be for such abuses to persist.

This is not to deny that the multinationals are in it for the money—and will strive to hire labour as cheaply as they can. But this does not appear to be a problem for the workers who compete to take those jobs. People who go to work for a foreign-owned company do so because they prefer it to the alternative, whatever that may be. In their own judgment, the new jobs make them better off.

But suppose for the moment that the sceptics are right, and that these workers, notwithstanding their own preferences, are victims of exploitation. One possibility would be to encourage foreign firms to pay higher wages in the third world. Another course, favoured by many sceptics, is to discourage multinationals from operating in the third world at all. But if the aim is to help the developing-country workers, this second strategy is surely wrong. If multinationals stopped hiring in the third world, the workers concerned would, on their own estimation, become worse off.

Compared with demands that the multinationals stay out of the third world altogether, the idea of merely shaming them into paying their workers higher wages seems a model of logic and compassion. Still, even this apparently harmless plan needs to be handled cautiously.

The question is, how much more is enough? At one extreme, you could argue that if a multinational company hires workers in developing countries for less than it pays their rich-country counterparts, it is guilty of exploitation. But to insist on parity would be tantamount to putting a stop to direct investment in the third world. By and large, workers in developing countries are paid less than workers in rich countries because they are less productive: those workers are attractive to rich-country firms, despite their lower productivity, because they are cheap. If you were to eliminate that offsetting advantage, you would make them unemployable.

Of course you could argue that decency merely requires multinationals to pay wages that are "fair," even if not on a par with wages in the industrial countries. Any mandatory increase in wages runs the risk of reducing the number of jobs created, but you could reply that the improvement in welfare for those who get the higher pay, so long as the mandated increase was moderate and feasible, would outweigh that drawback. Even then, however, two difficult questions would still need to be answered. What is a "fair" wage, and who is to decide?

What Fairness Requires

A "fair" wage can be deduced, you might argue, from economic principles: if workers are paid a wage that is less than their marginal productivity, you could say they are being exploited. Some sceptics regard it as obvious that third-world workers are being paid less than this. Their reasoning is that such workers are about as productive as their rich-country counterparts, and yet are paid only a small fraction of what rich-country workers receive. Yet there is clear evidence that third-world workers are not as productive as rich-country workers. Often they are working with less advanced machinery; and their productivity also depends on the surrounding economic infrastructure. More tellingly, though, if poor-country workers were being paid less than their marginal productivity, firms could raise their profits by hiring more of them in order to increase output. Sceptics should not need reminding that companies always prefer more profit to less.

Productivity aside, should "good practice" require, at least, that multinationals pay their poor-country employees more than other local workers? Not necessarily. To hire the workers they need, they may not have to offer a premium over local wages if they can provide other advantages. In any case, lack of a premium need not imply that they are failing to raise living standards. By entering the local labour market and adding to the total demand for labour, the multinationals would most likely be raising wages for all workers, not just those they hire.

In fact, though, the evidence suggests that multinationals do pay a wage premium—a reflection, presumably, of efforts to recruit relatively skilled workers. The wages paid by foreign affiliates to poor-country workers are about double the local manufacturing wage; wages paid by affiliates to workers in middle-income countries are about 1.8 times the local manufacturing wage (both calculations exclude wages paid to the firms' expatriate employees). The numbers come from calculations by Edward Graham at the Institute for International Economics. Mr. Graham cites other research which shows that wages in Mexico are highest near the border with the United States, where the operations of American-controlled firms are concentrated. Separate studies on Mexico, Venezuela, China and Indonesia have all found that foreign investors pay their local workers significantly better than other local employers.

Despite all this, you might still claim that the workers are not being paid a "fair" wage. But in the end, who is to make this judgment? The sceptics distrust governments, politicians, international bureaucrats and markets alike. So they end up appointing themselves as judges, overruling not just governments and markets but also the voluntary preferences of the workers most directly concerned. That seems a great deal to take on.

Globalization Does Not Harm Developing Nations' Cultures

by Tibor R. Machan

About the author: *Tibor R. Machan is a research fellow at the Hoover Institution on War, Revolution, and Peace and the editor of the book* Business Ethics in the Global Market.

Globalization, some say, is a form of imperialism. Along with the supposed invasiveness of American culture—via Hollywood movies, McDonald's hamburgers, and Coca-Cola products—globalization is seen by some as the equivalent of international aggression.

A similar charge was made some years ago at a United Nations conference in Vienna; representatives of some nondemocratic nations complained that the idea of human rights was intrusive and imperialistic and thus threatened the sovereignty of their countries. Some serious political thinkers still object to the very notion of universal ethical and political principles, as if human beings as such didn't share some basic attributes that imply certain guidelines for how they should live.

To charge that globalization is imperialistic is like claiming that liberating slaves imposes a particular lifestyle on the former slaves. Globalization, in its principled application, frees trade. Barriers are removed and restraint on trade is abolished, both the opposite of any kind of imposed imperialism.

The idea that economic principles are culturally relative confuses highly variable human practices with ones that are uniform across all borders. The production and exchange of goods and services are universal. The political contingencies of various societies, born often of power, not reason, distort such universality by imposing arbitrary impediments. Slavery, the subjugation of women, and the prohibition of wealth transfer from parents to offspring are examples of conditions not natural to human life—rather they are artifacts of ideologies.

American intellectuals often fail to appreciate the country's goal of establishing a political ideal for human beings in general, not for blacks, whites, women, Catholics, or Muslims. This ideal, when exported, is the farthest thing from imperialism. It is, in fact, the closest we have ever come to bona fide human liberation (a term inappropriately adopted by Marxists who mean to impose a one-size-fits-all regime).

"To charge that globalization is imperialistic is like claiming that liberating slaves imposes a particular lifestyle on the former slaves."

Globalization has thus not been effectively linked with what is at its heart, namely, human liberation. Because some schemes have been mislabeled as cases of "globalization," the genuine article has tended to acquire a bad reputation. But those are exceptions. To globalize has been to spread freedom, particularly in commerce but also in politics and civil life.

Genuine globalization should be supported not only because it is economically prudent but also because it is consistent with a basic human aspiration to be free. This is no threat to cultural diversity, religious pluralism, or the great variety of benign human differences with which globalization can happily coexist.

Only those who wish to impose their particular lifestyle on the rest of us would fear globalization and the spread of human freedom.

Chapter 3

Should Industrialized Nations Play an Active Role in the Developing World?

Chapter Preface

Aid to developing nations takes many forms. Some aid is in the form of direct monetary assistance—grants and loans aimed at stimulating developing nations' economies. For example, the United States provided roughly $10 billion in monetary aid to developing nations in 2000. A second, related form of aid is debt relief: the cancellation or restructuring (for example, lowering the interest rates) of previous loans. Government and charitable organizations also provide humanitarian aid to developing nations in times of crisis, sending shipments of food, clothing, and medical supplies, as well as groups of humanitarian aid workers. A fourth type of aid is aimed at promoting development in poor nations through primarily noneconomic means. For example, nations such as the United States may provide training to teachers or doctors; help build and run educational, medical, and sanitation facilities; or assist developing nations in conducting fair elections.

Economic aid does not just come from individual countries, but also from international organizations such as the United Nations, the World Bank, and the International Monetary Fund (IMF). The IMF and the World Bank were established in 1945 as independent agencies of the United Nations, whose purpose is to promote global economic cooperation. The World Bank is a lending institution, providing loans to developing nations; the IMF is the central policy-making institution of the international monetary system and is focused on managing exchange rates between nations and suggesting policies to avoid economic crises. More than 183 nations are members of the IMF and are, therefore, eligible for membership in the World Bank. These members provide the funding and governance of the World Bank and the IMF.

The loans and debt relief that wealthy nations and the World Bank provide are often tied to a developing country's agreement to enact economic, or sometimes political, reforms. Typically, the World Bank and the IMF require that nations receiving loans commit to "structural adjustment policies"—that is, reform their monetary, budgetary, market, and trade policies in ways that reduce government involvement in the economy and allow free markets to spur economic growth. Much of the controversy surrounding aid to developing nations concerns whether the aid should be tied to these structural adjustment policies, and if so, what these policies should be.

The authors in the following chapter explore the various controversies over foreign aid, debt relief, and the conditions often attached to them. At issue is not only the question of which policies will help developing nations the most, but also what role wealthier nations should play in influencing the development of poorer ones.

The United States Should Increase Its Efforts to Aid Developing Nations

by George W. Bush

About the author: *The following viewpoint is excerpted from a speech President George W. Bush gave at the United Nations Financing for Development Conference in Monterrey, Mexico, in March 2002.*

We meet at a moment of new hope and age-old struggle, the battle against world poverty. I'm honored to be with so many distinguished leaders who are committed to this cause. I'm here today to reaffirm the commitment of the United States to bring hope and opportunity to the world's poorest people, and to call for a new compact for development defined by greater accountability for rich and poor nations, alike.

I want to thank Vicente Fox, [the president of Mexico], and the people of Monterrey for such grand hospitality. I want to thank [United Nations secretary-general] Kofi Annan for his steadfast leadership. And I want to thank the distinguished leaders who are here for your hospitality, as well.

Many here today have devoted their lives to the fight against global poverty, and you know the stakes. We fight against poverty because hope is an answer to terror. We fight against poverty because opportunity is a fundamental right to human dignity. We fight against poverty because faith requires it and conscience demands it. And we fight against poverty with a growing conviction that major progress is within our reach.

The Millennium Challenge Account

Yet, this progress will require change. For decades, the success of development aid was measured only in the resources spent, not the results achieved. Yet, pouring money into a failed status quo does little to help the poor, and can actually delay the progress of reform. We must accept a higher, more difficult,

Excerpted from George W. Bush's speech delivered before the United Nations Financing for Development Conference in Monterrey, Mexico, March 22, 2002.

more promising call. Developed nations have a duty not only to share our wealth, but also to encourage sources that produce wealth: economic freedom, political liberty, the rule of law and human rights.

The lesson of our time is clear: When nations close their markets and opportunity is horded by a privileged few, no amount—no amount—of development aid is ever enough. When nations respect their people, open markets, invest in better health and education, every dollar of aid, every dollar of trade revenue and domestic capital is used more effectively.

We must tie greater aid to political and legal and economic reforms. And by insisting on reform, we do the work of compassion. The United States will lead by example. I have proposed a 50-percent increase in our core development assistance over the next three budget years. Eventually, this will mean a $5-billion annual increase over current levels.

These new funds will go into a new Millennium Challenge Account, devoted to projects in nations that govern justly, invest in their people and encourage economic freedom. We will promote development from the

> *"We fight against poverty with a growing conviction that major progress is within our reach."*

bottom up, helping citizens find the tools and training and technologies to seize the opportunities of the global economy.

I've asked Secretary of State Colin Powell, Secretary of Treasury Paul H. O'Neill to reach out to the world community to develop clear and concrete objective criterion for the Millennium Challenge Account. We'll apply these criterion fairly and rigorously.

And to jump-start this initiative, I'll work with the United States Congress to make resources available over the 12 months for qualifying countries. Many developing nations are already working hard on the road—and they're on the road of reform and bringing benefits to their people. The new Compact for Development will reward these nations and encourage others to follow their example.

The goal of our development aid will be for nations to grow and prosper beyond the need for any aid. When nations adopt reforms, each dollar of aid attracts two dollars of private investments. When aid is linked to good policy, four times as many people are lifted out of poverty compared to old aid practices.

All of us here must focus on real benefits to the poor, instead of debating arbitrary levels of inputs from the rich. We should invest in better health and build on our efforts to fight AIDS, which threatens to undermine whole societies. We should give more of our aid in the form of grants, rather than loans that can never be repaid.

More than Just Economic Aid

The work of development is much broader than development aid. The vast majority of financing for development comes not from aid, but from trade and domestic capital and foreign investment. Developing countries receive approximately $50 billion every year in aid. That is compared to foreign investment of almost $200 billion in annual earnings from exports of $2.4 trillion. So, to be serious about fighting poverty, we must be serious about expanding trade. Trade helped nations as diverse as South Korea and Chile and China to replace despair with opportunity for millions of their citizens. Trade brings new technology, new ideas and new habits, and trade brings ex-

> *"The vast majority of financing for development comes not from aid, but from trade and domestic capital and foreign investment."*

pectations of freedom. And greater access to the markets of wealthy countries has a direct and immediate impact on the economies of developing nations.

As one example, in a single year, the African Growth and Opportunity Act has increased African exports to the United States by more than 1,000 percent, generated nearly $1 billion in investment, and created thousands of jobs.

Yet we have much more to do. Developing nations need greater access to markets of wealthy nations. And we must bring down the high trade barriers between developing nations, themselves. The global trade negotiations launched in Doha [Quatar, in November 2001] confront these challenges.

The success of these negotiations will bring greater prosperity to rich and middle-income and poor nations alike. By one estimate, a new global trade pact could lift 300 million lives out of poverty. When trade advances, there's no question but the fact that poverty retreats.

The task of development is urgent and difficult, yet the way is clear. As we plan and act, we must remember the true source of economic progress is the creativity of human beings. Nations' most vital natural resources are found in the minds and skills and enterprise of their citizens. The greatness of a society is achieved by unleashing the greatness of its people. The poor of the world need resources to meet their needs, and like all people, they deserve institutions that encourage their dreams.

All people deserve governments instituted by their own consent; legal systems that spread opportunity, instead of protecting the narrow interests of a few; and the economic systems that respect their ambition and reward efforts of the people. Liberty and law and opportunity are the conditions for development, and they are the common hopes of mankind.

The spirit of enterprise is not limited by geography or religion or history. Men and women were made for freedom, and prosperity comes as freedom triumphs. And that is why the United States of America is leading the fight for freedom from terror.

We thank our friends and neighbors throughout the world for helping in this great cause. History has called us to a titanic struggle, whose stakes could not be higher because we're fighting for freedom itself. We're pursuing great and worthy goals to make the world safer, and as we do, to make it better. We will challenge the poverty and hopelessness and lack of education and failed governments that too often allow conditions that terrorists can seize and try to turn to their advantage.

Our new approach for development places responsibility on developing nations and on all nations. We must build the institutions of freedom, not subsidize the failures of the past. We must do more than just feel good about what we are doing, we must do good. By taking the side of liberty and good government, we will liberate millions from poverty's prison. We'll help defeat despair and resentment. We'll draw whole nations into an expanding circle of opportunity and enterprise. We'll gain true partners in development and add a hopeful new chapter to the history of our times.

May God bless you all.

Foreign Aid Benefits Developing Nations

by Michael J. Crosswell

About the author: *Michael J. Crosswell is an economist with the U.S. Agency for International Development (USAID), the agency of the federal government that extends assistance to developing nations.*

Critics of foreign aid like to argue that there has been little or no progress in the developing world. The Heritage Foundation's initial survey of economic freedom claimed: "Not only has U.S. development aid been wasted, it has actually retarded economic development in the countries that receive it. Not one country receiving foreign aid has succeeded in developing sustained economic growth." A more recent attack by the Cato Institute alleged that "few programs have consumed as many resources with as few positive results as foreign aid. . . . The recipients of that largesse have, by and large, failed to grow economically and develop democratically." On the basis of these sorts of claims, congressional critics have attacked foreign aid, complaining that "poor countries are still poor." Others might concede that economic growth has been achieved in parts of the developing world but argue that the poor have not benefited, owing to increased inequality in income. Some critics claim that few countries have graduated from foreign aid, and dependence on U.S. and other foreign assistance has been perpetuated. One prominent senator has argued that foreign aid has largely been poured down ratholes and is now an obsolete relic of the Cold War. (With this view of the role of foreign aid during the Cold War, why would one expect development progress?) Looking toward the future, these critics see only dim prospects for successful development, and little or no role at all for foreign aid.

Each of these arguments follows the same logical structure: recipients of foreign aid have failed to make development progress; therefore, foreign aid has failed. There is nothing wrong with the logic. If the premise held, the conclusion would follow.

Excerpted from "The Development Record and the Effectiveness of Foreign Aid," by Michael J. Crosswell, *U.S. Agency for International Development Bureau for Policy Program Coordination Staff Discussion Paper No. 1*, June 1998.

In point of fact, the premise is false. This viewpoint examines the extent of progress (and lack of progress) in development, paying particular attention to the sorts of criticisms cited above. It demonstrates that these critiques are largely without empirical foundation. Development performance on the whole has been positive, with much more success than failure, and much more progress than stagnation or decline. Prospects for further success are good.

Development progress does not by itself demonstrate the effectiveness of foreign aid. There is still the hypothetical possibility that while much progress has been made, foreign aid had little or nothing to do with it. More extensive analysis, including case studies, is needed to isolate the role of foreign aid.

Nonetheless, the fact of widespread development progress provides powerful *circumstantial* evidence for the effectiveness of foreign aid. And it clearly refutes the arguments made by the most politically prominent critics of foreign aid.

The Development Record

The findings in this viewpoint are based on an examination of the record *over the past three decades of 90 countries, currently inhabited by 3 billion people.* With one exception (South Africa), all were considered developing countries during the 1960s and 1970s, and all have been foreign aid recipients. Together they received $120 billion in U.S. bilateral economic aid during 1962–90. Since the explicit concern is with foreign aid recipients, the analysis excludes countries that were largely outside the sphere of development cooperation over the past three decades—such as China, the countries of Eastern Europe and the new independent states, Iran, Iraq, Lebanon, Libya, and Syria. Also excluded are numerous tiny countries, many of them islands.

Have foreign aid recipients been able to sustain economic growth? Readily available data offer both long-term and more recent perspectives on growth performance.

Looking at the period from 1965 to 1990, 41 countries, inhabited by more than 2.1 billion people, achieved significantly positive average annual rates of economic growth in per capita income, ranging from 1.3 to 8.4 percent. The average growth rate for these countries was 3.3 percent.

Of the remaining countries, some have realized greater success more recently. If we look at the period 1985–95, an additional 16 countries (280 million people) achieved significantly positive growth.

Combining the two groups, 57 out of 90 countries, embracing nearly 2.4

> *"The fact of widespread development progress provides powerful* **circumstantial** *evidence for the effectiveness of foreign aid."*

billion people (80 percent of the total population of 3 billion) have been able to sustain economic growth at meaningful rates for a reasonably long period of time.

Are poor countries still poor? Have poor countries failed to make economic progress? Of the 41 countries that achieved significant growth over the period 1965–90, most (25), accounting for 1.8 out of 2.1 billion people, were "poor" in 1965, using a per capita income criterion of $1,000 in 1990 prices. The average annual growth rate in per capita income for these countries was 3.5 percent. All of these countries have received large amounts of foreign aid, either in absolute terms or on a per capita basis. Of the 25, about half are now middle-income countries (using a $1,000 threshold), and several others are about to cross the threshold. . . .

> *"Some [foreign aid recipients] have joined the ranks of donor countries."*

What about graduation? At least 25 countries, inhabited by more than 675 million people, can be considered advanced (using economic and social indicators) and graduates with respect to dependence on foreign aid for development purposes. All were labeled developing countries in the 1960s, and as recently as the late 1970s; most received substantial amounts of foreign aid; and all are substantially independent of *developmental* foreign aid now. Some still receive aid, but for specific foreign policy purposes other than development—such as peace, narcotics, and global issues. Indeed, some have joined the ranks of donor countries, including Greece, Israel, Korea, Portugal, Singapore, Spain, Taiwan, Thailand, and Turkey.

Where Do We Stand Now?

The developing world is increasingly heterogeneous, with countries arrayed across a wide spectrum from relief to development to advanced status. From the standpoint of performance and progress over the past decade, the world can be divided into five large groups:

- *Advanced developing countries;* about 25 countries inhabited by 675 million people, which are (practically speaking) aid graduates, and in some cases have become donors.
- *Countries that are middle income, and where advanced status and graduation are not far off*, such as Botswana, the Dominican Republic, Ecuador, Egypt, El Salvador, Guatemala, Jamaica, Jordan, Morocco, Paraguay, Peru, the Philippines, South Africa, and Swaziland. This group includes about 260 million people and some major aid recipients. Most should be expected to achieve advanced status and graduate over the next decade or so.
- *Countries that are by and large still poor but have made significant economic progress over the past decade or longer*, with average annual growth rates in per capita income ranging from 1.3 to 6.0 percent. These include Bangladesh, Bolivia, Ghana, India, Indonesia, Mozambique, Nepal, Pakistan, Sri Lanka, Uganda, and Vietnam. Together they account for about 1.5 billion people and two thirds of global poverty (not counting China). Their prospects for continued growth are good, but in many instances fragile, as

evidenced most vividly by Pakistan. Continued progress in this group would mean major reductions in global poverty.

• *Poor countries making at best intermittent progress.* These include most of sub-Saharan Africa, plus a small number of countries such as Cambodia, Haiti, Honduras, Nicaragua, and Yemen. This group of 40 countries accounts for 570 million people, less than one fifth of the total population of the 90 countries under review here, and less than the population of the group of advanced countries.

A subset would be countries in crisis or stalemate—including Afghanistan, Burma, Congo, Liberia, Rwanda, Somalia, Sudan—about 160 million people. These are the countries most commonly cited in critiques of foreign aid. However, they are only a small part of the bigger picture. Overall, this group can be seen as the last frontier for development progress. Social indicators have improved in most cases, but institutional capabilities are still weak, and economic progress has been limited and sporadic. Most of these countries started the development race from a position of relative and absolute backwardness, particularly in terms of institutional capabilities and human resources. The challenge here is to move from "at best intermittent" to "steady" progress, including the move from relief to development for countries in crisis.

• *The transitional postcommunist countries.* These 25 or so countries, home to about 400 million people, are arguably off the "third world" continuum described above. Indeed, they embody their own continuum, covering a wide spectrum of economic performance and prospects; income, poverty, and human resource development; and proximity to graduation. The predominant challenge in these transitional countries is one of discarding and replacing "maldeveloped" (rather than underdeveloped) institutions, both economic and political. The foreign aid track record in these countries is considerably shorter, but there has already been some success, including recent and prospective graduation.

> *"Maintaining momentum in the very populous group of poor countries that have made clear, steady progress would constitute major success."*

If we look at these groups over time, we see that most of the countries that are "ahead" in 1997 were ahead in 1965. Those that have made the least progress are by and large those that were the least developed in 1965. For instance, the top 26 countries in terms of *1965* per capita income include 22 of the countries considered graduates in the tally above. (Only Colombia, Thailand, and Tunisia moved up into the top group.) Remaining countries in the middle-income group that are poised for graduation over the next decade or so were mostly in the middle of the pack in 1965. Finally, of the 51 countries that are considered "poor" today (the third and fourth groups), all but 7 were in the bottom 50 in 1965.

These considerations help debunk some of the less informed characterizations of foreign aid that have emanated from conservative think tanks. These critics often compare advanced countries receiving little aid with poor countries receiving larger amounts of aid, and conclude that aid retards development. Similarly, they portray development progress as *purely* a function of political will, ignoring the wide disparities in initial conditions, including human resources and institutional capabilities, that are critical to development progress. For example, the Heritage Foundation has compared Hong Kong with Tanzania, arguing that Hong Kong received relatively little aid and has made great progress, while Tanzania has received a great deal of aid and is still poor. This ignores the huge initial differences between Hong Kong and Tanzania in the early 1960s in terms of human resource development and institutional capabilities, as represented by per capita income 22 times higher in Hong Kong than in Tanzania in 1965, and similarly large gaps in social indicators. . . .

Continued Progress

Looking ahead, there is plenty of room to build on this record, including substantial progress in reducing global poverty and in graduation, *simply by maintaining recent trends.* In particular, achieving advanced status and graduation in the middle-income group, and maintaining momentum in the very populous group of poor countries that have made clear, steady progress would constitute major success. The goal, of course, is not simply to maintain trends but to improve them, particularly in the group of poor countries that have made only intermittent progress. In support of this goal, there is a good and increasing knowledge base about the requisites for development progress—especially human resource development, sound policies, and improved institutions—based on successful experience. There is increasing consensus on what constitutes good policies and institutions, and mounting awareness of which countries are making adequate self-help efforts. With globalization, the rewards for good policies and strengthened institutions and the costs of poor policies and weak institutions are increasingly large and visible.

The predominantly successful development record does not prove the effectiveness of foreign aid. But it provides powerful, positive circumstantial evidence. And it refutes the sorts of claims cited in the introduction. Critics who want to continue to make the case that foreign aid has been ineffective need to consider more carefully the evidence on development performance, and create arguments that do not rest on gross mischaracterizations of the development record.

Debt Relief Can Help Developing Nations Overcome Poverty

by the Catholic Fund for Overseas Development

About the author: *The Catholic Fund for Overseas Development (CAFOD) is a major British charity that has been fighting poverty in developing nations since 1962.*

The 1970s started out with a great deal of promise for the Third World, for Africa in particular. Commodity prices were buoyant and growth prospects good. But oil price hikes in 1973 and 1979 led to hyperinflation in industrialised countries, whose response included steep rises in interest rates. The net effect in the North was economic recession and a slump in demand for commodity exports from the South. So southern governments borrowed [from northern governments, the World Bank, and the International Monetary Fund (IMF)] to make up for their revenue shortfalls on the assumption that the economic downturn would be short-lived. And they took on loans at floating interest rates, borrowing initially at a low rate and then having to service their debts at rates four or five times higher.

These new debts also had to be repaid in US dollars. With interest rates rising in the North and a slump in exports in the South, debtor governments saw their export revenue dwindle. At the same time, their debt grew daily as the dollar increased in value and interest rates soared even higher.

By the late 1970s and 1980s, the accumulation of the poorest countries' debts had become unsustainable.

The deteriorating global economy was one factor in the debt crisis, but many debtor governments share some of the responsibility. Most were wedded to a centralised model of economic management. There were bottlenecks in production, private indigenous enterprise was discouraged, exports shrank and economic growth was stifled. Many governments borrowed for glamorous, but ultimately unproductive, large-scale projects.

Creditor governments were also to blame. They wanted to create employment at home, so they lent southern governments the money to buy goods from their own countries. They also lent to their Cold War allies in the Third World: some of the more corrupt governments, such as that of President Mobutu in Zaire, received loans from western governments, the IMF and World Bank. Irresponsible lending and borrowing was also common among Soviet bloc allies. Proliferating Cold War conflicts also encouraged political lending on both sides—the priority was to win friends and influence, regardless of the economic value of the loans.

The spiralling costs of debt repayment and servicing, combined with contracting economies, led the most heavily indebted and poorest countries to default on their debts. Eventually this produced an unpayable mountain of arrears. By the mid-1980s, debt and deepening poverty constituted a humanitarian disaster for many of the poorest countries. During the past two decades the world's most heavily indebted continent, Africa, has experienced falling incomes and investment, falling life expectancies and rising infant and maternal mortality rates. Debt has become not only an economic issue, but a matter of life and death.

The world's poorest countries were in effect bankrupt. But the international economic order does not allow countries to sue for insolvency and start again. Governments were largely content to ignore the plight of the poorest in faraway countries. It was only the efforts of debt campaigners the world over that challenged the reasoning of creditors.

Debt Relief Begins

Throughout the late 1980s and early 1990s, creditor governments, the IMF and the World Bank argued that the problem of debtor countries was one of short-term financing and that the debts were not an obstacle to poverty reduction.

The IMF and World Bank said the outflow of resources in the form of debt repayments was offset by a larger inflow in the form of aid or new loans. In other words, donors and creditors were keeping debtor governments afloat with regular top-ups of new aid and lending.

In the late 1980s, richer governments conceded that poorer countries needed some debt relief. Creditor governments, grouped in the so-called Paris Club, devised a series of concessions named after the cities where they met: London dealt with commercial debts; Toronto, Houston, Lyon, and Naples eventually offered relief on up to 67 per cent of debt. But this debt relief was limited in scope. Naples terms offered to write off 67 per cent of the debt owed to governments at the time the debtor country first approached the Paris Club for relief—the so-called cut-off date. Any new borrowing, to pay off interest on old debts or to buy essential imports, would have to be repaid in full.

This piecemeal approach failed to address the growing mountain of debt owed to the World Bank and IMF. A single framework was needed to deal comprehensively with all creditors.

Chapter 3

Debt Relief Continues—the HIPC Initiative

Aid agencies, and later the Jubilee 2000 campaign, argued that the debt problem was not merely a narrow issue of countries defaulting on their debts. It was, and still is, a problem of social justice. The agencies argued that it was unacceptable that those who could afford the least were paying—literally with their lives—those who already had the most.

In 1996, the creditors responded to public pressure with the Heavily Indebted Poor Country (HIPC) initiative. In response to the Jubilee 2000 campaign's impatience with the meagre results, in 1999 they made marginal improvements in the form of an "enhanced HIPC initiative".

For the first time the world's poorest countries were promised debt cancellation so that they could achieve "a robust exit from the burden of unsustainable debts".

Moreover, in 1999 the G8 Summit in Cologne acknowledged that unsustainable or unpayable debt was a serious obstacle to poverty reduction.

From then on, all creditors were to share equally the cost of writing off the debts of qualifying countries. And their debts were to be reduced until they became "sustainable".

How Much Debt Has Been Cancelled?

Calculating how much debt relief debtor countries have received is not an exact science. There are various ways of determining the amount a country owes—the value of the debts when they were first taken out, or their value in debt markets, or their value at current prices when interest has been added. On the last measure, most commentators agree that writing off the debts of the 24 countries that have gone through the HIPC process will cost creditors about US$36 billion.

This sounds impressive. But from the point of view of debtor countries, it seems far less generous. Because most debtor governments did not, and could not, keep up their repayments, most of the US$36 billion consists of interest and principal they had not been repaying and were never going to repay. On average, the initiative will cut the HIPCs' expenditure on debt servicing by one third.

"By the mid-1980s, debt and deepening poverty constituted a humanitarian disaster for many of the poorest countries."

For example, Mozambique was paying about US$120 million a year in interest and principal. After debt reduction, the country will continue to spend more than US$70 million a year in debt service. The reduction in Tanzania's annual debt service will only be about ten per cent. Cameroon and Zambia, where one in every five children does not live to see their fifth birthday and their parents earn less than 60 cents a day each, will be left with a combined debt stock of nearly US$5 billion.

What's Wrong with HIPC?

The generous view is that the enhanced HIPC initiative has simply failed to meet both of its objectives—to reduce debt to sustainable levels and to produce sufficient additional finance to reduce poverty. In reality, the rules governing the application of the HIPC initiative are often broken and inconsistently applied.

The system is supposed to be transparent about who qualifies for debt reduction and how much they will get. But two countries that do not meet the eligibility criteria—Bolivia and Honduras—are in. And some that do meet the requirements—Cambodia, Georgia, Haiti and Afghanistan—are out. Others that have been excluded—for example, Nigeria—have no prospect of developing without debt reduction. Pakistan received debt relief in return for assisting the US and its allies after [the] 11 September 2001 [terrorist attacks on America], although it is clearly ineligible under both Paris Club and HIPC rules.

Also, the calculation of how much debt relief countries should get is elastic. Before 1999, debt reduction was given if total debt was more than twice a country's export earnings. After lobbying by the Jubilee 2000 campaign, this threshold was reduced to 1.5 times a country's export earnings.

At first, IMF officials argued that there was "absolutely no analytical justification" for this reduction. When reminded of this position in meetings, they justified the extra debt relief as a "cushion effect" in case a country's export earnings fell after it received debt relief.

Other problems with the HIPC initiative include:

- Some bilateral creditors write off only the debts acquired before HIPCs first approached their creditors for debt relief. Some countries first appealed for help in the mid-1980s. Twenty years later, they are being offered 100 per cent relief on those original sums only, but not on any subsequent borrowing. So headlines of "100 per cent debt relief!" can be misleading.

- The World Bank and IMF decide how much debt should be cancelled. But the figures they use for their calculations depend on hopelessly optimistic forecasts about future export earnings, growth and aid inflows. This significantly reduces the relief given and countries have to return to the negotiating table when the figures are proved wrong.

> *"[The debt crisis] was, and still is, a problem of social justice."*

- After receiving debt relief, HIPCs need to continue borrowing to keep up their debt servicing obligations and to cover their foreign exchange outgoings—purchase of essential imports, for example. So even by the definition of "sustainability" used by the World Bank and the IMF, their debts are unpayable.

- To qualify for HIPC debt relief, governments must adopt economic policies prescribed by the creditors. This works against poor people, because governments are required to cut subsidies and other spending that benefits the poor.

As one Zambian finance ministry official put it: "We introduced the economic reforms and reduced inflation quicker than the Nazis and still our poverty levels are rising." In theory, free-market reforms will eventually lead to increased economic growth, but the poor have yet to experience any benefit.

Debt and Poverty

The fundamental weakness of the HIPC initiative is that it uses narrow financial criteria to judge how much debt to write off, and ignores poverty indicators. Assessing whether a country can afford to pay its debts by looking only at its export earnings is wholly inappropriate for low-income countries. For economies that are dependent on one or two export commodities, such as coffee or cocoa, and are prone to droughts that can drastically decrease their export income, gauging debt sustainability from projections of export revenue is foolhardy, misguided and usually wrong.

"There is growing evidence that debt relief immediately benefits economic growth."

This is not only an unreliable way of predicting the sustainability of debt. It is also at odds with the requirement that debtor governments should draw up poverty reduction plans to show how they will use the resources freed by debt relief to tackle poverty. The amount of debt relief a country receives has nothing to do with the cost of those plans or the levels of poverty it has to tackle.

In defence of the HIPC initiative, creditors have argued both ways. On the one hand, they maintain that its purpose is to fund poverty reduction. On the other, they assert that the purpose of the initiative is to make debt sustainable in the more narrow financial sense. In reality, it fails in both.

Will More Aid Solve the Problem?

When this failure is pointed out, creditors argue that new aid will finance poverty reduction. But this argument has serious flaws.

- In practice, donors avoid coordinating with each other. As a result, recipient country civil servants are left negotiating, reporting and conducting audits on a range of programmes when their time would be better spent improving their own administration. Tanzania, for instance, has to produce more than 800 reports each quarter to over 50 donors.
- Often donors shape their aid programmes according to their own strategic interests rather than the recipient countries' needs. France, for instance, is willing to spend large amounts of "aid" money promoting French culture. The US prefers to give to allies—Egypt, Poland and Israel—rather than to the poorest countries. Japan prefers to give aid that boosts its exports. In 2001 Britain provided export credit guarantees for a £28 million military radar system for Tanzania, when a £7 million civil aviation radar system would have served just as well. This appears more effective at sustaining

jobs in the United Kingdom than at meeting needs in Tanzania.

- All donors—except the United States—have agreed to increase their aid spending to 0.7 per cent of Gross National Product (GNP). In more than 30 years since the UN adopted this target, aid expenditure—as a proportion of donor country incomes—has declined steeply.
- Unlike debt relief, aid flows are highly unpredictable and often hamper governments' efforts at medium-term planning.

Debt relief, unlike aid, immediately reduces the outflow of funds, and, by bolstering governments' budgets, supports their spending on poverty reduction. And there is growing evidence that debt relief immediately benefits economic growth.

The Way Forward

According to Catholic Social Teaching, economic policy-making should have at its centre the needs and rights of the least advantaged in society. So far, creditors have approached debt relief on the basis of what they are willing to pay, rather than what debtor countries need.

CAFOD argues that governments must prioritise poverty reduction and basic human development. Only when such programmes are fully funded—from tax revenues, development aid and the proceeds of debt reduction—should any remaining resources be allocated to debt service.

If the international community is serious about achieving the internationally agreed development goal of halving global poverty by 2015, it must rethink its policies on debt. A significant group of countries, mostly in Africa, is likely to miss the 2015 development targets because of a lack of finance. The amount of debt that can be repaid by each country should be judged according to the additional finance required to achieve these targets. For many, this will mean 100 per cent cancellation of their outstanding debts by the rich-country governments, the World Bank and the IMF.

The world's poorest countries are pushing for this human development approach to calculating debt sustainability. They want the criteria for assessing the extent of debt relief to focus on poverty levels. In the UN and the World Bank, they have called for debt reduction that will provide the financial resources they need to reduce poverty.

But the richest creditors are using their majority shareholding in the World Bank and the IMF to resist this demand. Is it fair that global institutions make their decisions in this way?

Fair and Transparent Arbitration

The debt crisis has lasted for more than 25 years at enormous cost to the lives of the poorest and most vulnerable people. Creditors have long taken a half-hearted approach to the problem, and then only after pressure from debt campaigners. Even though most independent commentators agree that the HIPC initiative is not solving the problem, the global financial authorities, controlled by the richest countries, are refusing to budge.

Currently, creditors control the pace, amount and criteria for relief. Because creditors act as prosecutor, judge and jury in assessing how much debt relief should be made available, campaigners argue, the results will always be unfair or inadequate.

They argue that a fair and transparent arbitration process should be developed to decide how much debt relief countries need. All stakeholders, and in particular the civil society representatives of the affected countries, have a right to be heard. And to protect the basic needs of the poor in debtor countries, there should be an automatic stay of debt servicing once a country asks for debt relief.

According to CAFOD's partner in Zambia, Mulima Kufekisa Akapelwa:

"If the people in the heavily indebted poor countries are always going to be excluded from the talks which determine their future, then we are doubtful that the decisions taken on their behalf will be just ones.

"We are now saying the people of the South must be included in the discussions that decide their fate."

The United States Should Support Family Planning Services in Developing Nations

by Ann Hwang

About the author: *At the time this viewpoint was written, Ann Hwang was a medical student at the University of California, San Francisco.*

The "global gag rule" is stifling debate about reproductive health. It's going to force a lot of poor women in developing countries to bear children they don't want. It's likely to increase (not decrease) the number of "coat hanger" abortions. And it's probably going to get a lot of women killed, which will in turn boost death rates among the children they leave behind. So why exactly is it U.S. policy?

The desire to control fertility may be nearly as ancient and universal as sexual desire itself. Every culture, it seems, has had its contraceptives, although their efficacy has varied greatly. To prevent pregnancy, the Petrie Papyrus, an Egyptian medical text from 1850 BC, recommended vaginal suppositories made of crocodile dung. In the 4th century BC, Aristotle described women coating their cervixes with olive oil before intercourse. Women on Easter Island made suppositories from seaweed. And from the 1930s to the 1960s, Lysol, now a popular household cleaner, was marketed coyly to American women as a "certain . . . yet safe" disinfectant douche.

The Need for Family Planning Services

In the developing world today, nearly two-thirds of all women in their reproductive years—about 525 million of them—rely on some form of birth control, according to the United Nations Population Fund (UNFPA). But there is still a great deal of unmet demand for contraceptives. More than 100 million women in these countries say they want to delay the birth of their next child or stop having children altogether, but are not currently using contraception.

Family planning has been recognized by the international community as a fundamental human right. Under the program of action adopted at the International Conference on Population and Development in Cairo in 1994, "All couples and individuals have the basic right to decide freely and responsibly the number and spacing of their children [that is, the length of time between births] and to have the information, education, and means to do so." But efforts to secure this right were dealt a serious setback in 2001. On his first working day and the 28th anniversary of the U.S. Supreme Court decision that legalized abortion in the United States, President George W. Bush issued an executive order that resurrected a measure known informally as the "global gag rule."

Essentially, the gag rule prohibits foreign family planning organizations from receiving U.S. government aid if they provide abortions (except in cases of rape, incest, or danger to a woman's life), or if they counsel women about abortion as an option for dealing with an unwanted pregnancy, or if they advocate less restrictive abortion laws in their own countries. The restrictions apply even if no U.S. funding is being used for the activities in question: any such activities, no matter how they are funded, render an organization ineligible for U.S. support. The gag rule, which obviously gets its common name from its sanctions against free speech, had first been imposed by Ronald Reagan in 1984. Bill Clinton lifted the policy during his first week in office. Its reinstatement by Bush has put the United States in a peculiar diplomatic position: while formally committed to the Cairo program of action, the United States is in effect using its economic power to undermine the human rights principle upon which the program is built.

The U.S. government is the largest international donor to family planning programs. U.S. contributions flow through the country's foreign aid agency, the U.S. Agency for International Development (USAID), which has budgeted $425 million for family planning for the 2002 fiscal year. About half of this money will go to foreign governments and to multilateral agencies like UNFPA, to whom the gag rule does not apply. The other half will be channeled to non-governmental organizations (NGOs), which are subject to the rule.

The rule applies on a rolling basis: when a project is due for renewal, the managing organization must decide whether to comply or forgo funding.

"Family planning has been recognized by the international community as a fundamental human right."

USAID supports medical training and research on family planning, but it also funds the direct provision of services to millions of couples in over 60 countries, including many of the poorest and most densely populated on Earth. In comparison to other major international donors, USAID relies heavily on

NGOs to carry out its family planning activities. And that makes U.S. programs highly vulnerable to the gag rule.

The effects of the rule are already being felt. The compliance option has been rejected by two of the largest international providers of reproductive health services, the International Planned Parenthood Federation (IPPF) and Marie Stopes International (MSI, named after the activist who in 1921 founded the first British family planning clinic). These organizations argue that as a matter of principle, they cannot exclude access to safe abortion from the set of reproductive health goals that they are trying to advance. As a result, IPPF will lose approximately $8 million from 2001 to 2003, or 8 percent of its budget; MSI has thus far lost over $2 million. To date, at least a half dozen other NGOs—some international and some local—have lost funding by refusing to comply with the gag rule.

The potential consequences led Anthony Browne, health editor of the British newspaper, the *Observer*, to label the gag rule "the Bush edict that kills women." Clinic closures have already been reported from Nepal to Peru to Kenya. Marie Stopes-Kenya, for example, has closed two centers serving the slums of Nairobi and Kisumi. In Kenya as a whole, only one in four married women uses a modern method of contraception, according to UNFPA. In the poor areas served by these clinics, the proportion is likely to be even lower. The country also has a high maternal mortality rate: for every 100,000 births, 650 women die as a consequence of pregnancy or childbirth. One-third of those deaths are caused by botched abortions, even though Kenya has restrictive abortion laws.

> *"In depriving access to . . . basic reproductive health choices, . . . Mr. Bush has condemned more women to . . . resort to desperate, life-threatening methods to abort."*

The pervasiveness of abortion, even where it is illegal or cannot be safely performed, is perhaps the clearest indication of the gag rule's medical absurdity. The rule's ostensible objective is to reduce the number of abortions, but by obstructing the delivery of family planning services as a whole, it is likely to have just the opposite effect. As Sue Newport, MSI's Africa Regional Director, explains, "In depriving access to contraception and basic reproductive health choices through these unavoidable clinic closures, Mr. Bush has condemned more women to face crisis pregnancies and resort to desperate, life-threatening methods to abort."

The rule is a legal absurdity as well. In the first place, it's discriminatory because it applies to pro-choice activities only: anti-abortion lobbying does not render an organization ineligible for funding. The rule also sends a strong signal to developing countries that the United States disapproves of abortion; that will likely set back efforts to increase access to safe abortion, despite the fact that in the United States, abortion is legal. In developing countries that permit abortion, the rule has the bizarre effect of preventing counselors from discussing a procedure allowed by law; with the very people most likely to need it. More generally, the rule's suppression of debate is hardly a proud reflection of the U.S. constitution, which is supposed to guarantee the right of free speech. Susana Galdos Silva, an activist for the Movimiento Manuela Ramos, a Peruvian women's rights NGO that accepts USAID money and has consequently been gagged, testified on this matter at a U.S. Senate hearing in July 2001. "The gag rule," she said, "has taken away my freedom to speak about an important issue in my country—a serious issue that is about the life and death of women in Peru." Had it been delivered in Peru, her testimony would itself have been sufficient to disqualify her organization for U.S. aid. Some critics of the rule regard such de facto censorship as a kind of ideological hegemony. Malcolm Potts, Bixby professor of population and family planning at the University of California, Berkeley, School of Public Health, puts it this way: "You can't run a world on a few people's political and religious assertions."

No Family Planning, No Security

Family planning provides a higher return on investment than almost any other type of development assistance. "A development success story" is the phrase the World Bank used in its 1994 survey of the field. Its most obvious successes appear, not in demographic trends, but in the lives of the women it reaches. In the developing world, pregnancy and childbirth are the leading cause of death and disability for women of reproductive age. Worldwide, UNFPA estimates that over 500,000 women die in pregnancy or childbirth each year and several million more suffer injury or infection. Ninety-eight percent of these women live in developing countries. In Africa, the continent with the highest rates of maternal death, a woman has a one in sixteen chance of dying in childbirth over her lifetime. Before giving birth, African mothers sometimes bid their older children farewell. In Tanzania, a common formula is: "I am going to the sea to fetch a new baby but the journey is long and dangerous."

The World Health Organization estimates that 100,000 maternal deaths could be avoided each year if all women who said they wanted to stop bearing children were able to do so. Reducing maternal mortality would also confer enormous benefits on large numbers of children, as is apparent in a negative way from current child mortality statistics: in some developing countries, the loss of a mother increases the death rate by 50 percent for children under the age of five.

For most couples, family planning might best be characterized not as a way of preventing pregnancy outright, but as a way of better managing its frequency. Spacing births at least two years apart leaves time for a mother's body to recover, allows more attention to be given to the newborn, and tends to improve nutrition for both mother and child. The result is a 50 percent increase in infant survival.

The benefits of family planning extend well beyond the health effects. There is a strong correlation between lower fertility rates and the educational and financial advancement of women. This correlation was borne out, for example, by an 11-year study of working women in Cebu city in the Philippines. Researchers found that the fewer children a woman had, the greater the increase in her earnings over that period. Although it is difficult to distinguish cause from effect in such situations, few if any experts doubt that family planning improves the social position of women.

At the national level, reducing population growth can promote economic development. Some economists argue that families with fewer children save more money, a phenomenon called the "demographic bonus." Higher savings rates may in turn reduce a country's dependence on foreign capital. Decreasing population growth can also ease the strain on overtaxed natural resources, particularly those associated with subsistence agriculture. Today, an estimated 420 million people live in countries where the amount of cropland per capita has dropped below 0.07 hectares—the amount generally deemed necessary to sustain a bare minimum vegetarian diet. By 2025, the number of people living in such countries will probably have reached between 550 million and 1 billion. But the most important limit is not likely to be access to land; it's likely to be access to water. Already, half a billion people are living in areas prone to severe water shortages. In 25 years, that number will probably have risen to between 2.4 and 3.2 billion.

Such figures suggest the importance of family planning as a global enterprise. By 2050, the world's population is likely to approach 9 billion—almost a 50 percent increase from its current level of 6.1 billion. Nearly all of that increase will come in the developing world and at this point, most of it is probably inevitable. That's because record numbers of young people are now coming into their peak reproductive years (between the ages of 15 and 24). Even if the global fertility rate (the average number of children per woman) were to fall overnight from its current level of 2.8 to the longterm "replacement level" of 2.1, more than three-quarters of the growth projected for the next half century would still occur, because of the enormous demographic bulge of young adults.

This population expansion will create profound challenges to development in many ways—political, technical, and moral. Family planning is going to be essential for managing those challenges. On this broad demographic level, family planning could be said to serve two purposes: incremental reduction of population growth over the relatively near term, and over the long term, ensuring that the growth actually stops somewhere around that 9 billion mark.

The Decency Gap

The gag rule is a product of American neoconservatism. Hostility to family planning was not a standard element in the conservative outlook before the Reagan era. In 1969, with the United States firmly committed to providing family planning assistance overseas, it did not seem incongruous to hear President Richard Nixon identify population growth as "one of the most serious challenges to human destiny in the last third of this century."

But the election of Ronald Reagan in 1980 inaugurated a marked shift in both conservative ideology and the electoral mechanics of the Republican Party. During Reagan's presidency, conservative Christianity became an increasingly influential force within the party. And of course, the issue that conservative Christian groups care most about— then and now—is abortion, which they want to outlaw. Their position on family planning proper (which is built around the provision of contraceptives, not abortion) varies somewhat but is generally unfavorable.

"Hostility to family planning was not a standard element in the conservative outlook before the Reagan era."

This constituency scored a major coup at the 1984 population conference in Mexico City, when the Reagan administration announced that it had adopted the initial version of the gag rule as U.S. policy. (The rule is still sometimes called the Mexico City policy.)

Opposition to family planning picked up additional momentum from serious abuses within several national programs. Coercive government policies have sometimes created a lasting suspicion of family planning in the countries concerned; this happened in parts of India, for example, after the forced sterilization programs in the mid-1970s under the Indira Gandhi administration. In Washington, such cases of coercion have tended to strengthen the neoconservative agenda. In 1985, the Reagan administration expressed its displeasure with China's one-child policy, which has been associated with forced sterilizations and forced abortions, by ordering a $10 million cut in U.S. contributions to UNFPA. The cut was equal to the amount that UNFPA was spending on Chinese family planning programs. (Despite its involvement in China, UNFPA does not endorse any form of compulsion.) In the following year, U.S. support for UNFPA was eliminated altogether. (It was not restored until 1993 and even today, the United States continues to deduct from its contribution an amount equal to UNFPA's China expenditures.) In 1998, accounts of forced sterilization in Peru triggered U.S. legislation withholding monetary and food aid to that country until the sterilization program was stopped.

The Reagan era gag rule set off a series of reactions that substantially undercut family planning efforts in the developing world. Two of the field's biggest "umbrella organizations," IPPF and the affiliated Family Planning International Assistance, decided that they couldn't comply, and consequently lost funding. IPPF lost a full quarter of its operating budget. Out in the field, the efforts of many little NGOs—the "sub-grantees" under these umbrellas—were disrupted by the cuts. In the schools, educational curricula were purged of references to abortion; medical textbooks mentioning the subject were withdrawn. And although post-abortion services were not explicitly prohibited, the rule reportedly had a chilling effect on both the providers and seekers of this type of care.

Meanwhile in Washington, the gag rule's supporters were looking beyond the rule itself. In 1985, USAID granted funds to the Family of the Americas Foundation, an organization opposed to all artificial methods of birth control. This grant violated USAID's own informed consent policy, which requires family planning programs to supply information on all contraceptive methods.

Even after Bill Clinton repealed the gag rule, Congress continued to use its power over the budget to chip away at family planning expenditures. From its peak of $542 million in fiscal year 1995, Congress cut USAID funding for family planning by 35 percent for the next fiscal year—a substantially greater loss than the 20 percent cut inflicted on foreign aid as a whole. The family planning budget regained some ground in the following year but in 1999, Clinton struck a deal with congressional conservatives: in exchange for an agreement to pay back dues owed to the United Nations, Clinton signed a more lenient version of the gag rule, which cut USAID funding by $12.5 million. Late in his presidency, Clinton negotiated a 2001 budget with ostensibly more favorable terms. Family planning funding would be increased to $425 million and the gag rule withdrawn—but conservatives insisted on one important condition: no funds could be disbursed until after February 15, 2001. Thus the fate of the rule hinged on what turned out to be one of the most unusual presidential elections in American history.

Bush lost no time in reinstating the rule with all its Reagan-era restrictions, but the intervening 17 years had altered the field. In the first place, there are more NGOs than there used to be, particularly in the advocacy sector. NGOs are also generally better organized and more sophisticated—

"Most Americans appear to know little about population issues."

and USAID is much more dependent upon them to drive its family planning programs. Abortion laws have changed too: in many countries, restrictions have eased, so compliance with the gag rule will probably be more onerous than it once was. Overall, these changes are liable to make the effects of the rule more complex than in the 1980s. More complex means less predictable, but it's safe to say that in many developing countries, civil society is much less likely simply to accept the gag.

In the short term, at least, the rule's effects will probably be mitigated somewhat by funding increases from elsewhere. Foul Nielson, the European commissioner for development, announced his commitment to fill the immediate funding shortfall, which he called "the decency gap." In June, both the Danish and the Finnish governments increased their IPPE contributions. And *Los Angeles Times* columnist Patt Morrison sparked an informal fundraising campaign in the United States, when she told readers she was planning to make a donation to Planned Parenthood in George W. Bush's name as a President's Day "gift." Her idea, circulated over the internet, brought in tens of thousands of contributions. . . .

Does the Gag Rule Have Momentum?

The resurrection of the gag rule suggests that attacks on family planning may escalate. Although Bush insists that he supports family planning itself, conservative policy appears to be singling the field out for unfavorable treatment. This is apparent, in the first place, from the way the rule itself works. The rule does not restrict USAID funding for HIV prevention, safe motherhood, or child survival programs, even though these activities overlap significantly with family planning—for example, in the distribution of condoms—and even though many of the same NGOs are involved. Only family planning comes in for the gag rule's restrictions. As development policy, such contradictions don't seem to make much sense. But as a U.S. domestic political strategy, unfortunately, they do: to many conservative political activists, family planning is suspect; safe motherhood and other such programs are not. . . .

Conservatives have also been targeting [domestic] family planning proper. Bush's proposed budget for 2001 eliminated coverage of contraceptives from the federal employee health insurance plan. Congress overruled him on this point, but Congress itself may be undermining contraception in a less controversial way. For the 2001 fiscal year, Congress approved a $20 million increase in funding for abstinence-only sex education programs, and a $30 million increase for 2002. But no increase has been approved for family planning. The goal, say officials, is to spend as much money on abstinence-only programs as on family planning, despite the fact that the latter provides medical services and supplies, while abstinence-only programs consist mostly of classes and workshops. Nor is there any evidence that abstinence-only programs actually work.

Attacks on domestic family planning are bad news for the international programs, which are likely to be even more vulnerable to politicians out to prove their commitment to some "pro-life" constituency. That vulnerability is probably in part the result of ignorance: most Americans appear to know little about population issues. A recent survey by the RAND Corporation, a nonprofit policy think rank, found that only 14 percent of the U.S. population had even a rough sense of what the global population is. They estimated it at about 5 to 6 billion—but a similar proportion of the people surveyed thought it was greater than 30 billion! Yet despite their fuzziness on the reasons why it is needed, Americans seem to have little problem with family planning per se. The RAND survey found that 80 percent of Americans favor support of voluntary family planning programs in developing countries. Apparently, then, the gag rule is not taking U.S. policy in a direction that most Americans would want it go. And it is certainly not taking it in the direction envisioned by the Cairo conference—towards a world with fewer abortions, healthier mothers, and healthier babies.

The United States Should Not Increase Foreign Aid to Developing Nations

by Steve Bonta

About the author: *Steve Bonta is a writer for the* New American, *a biweekly conservative magazine.*

America sends billions of taxpayer dollars overseas in the form of foreign aid. Yet more often than not the money ends up aiding oppressive regimes and our nation's enemies.

On May 17th [2001], Secretary of State Colin Powell announced a new $43 million aid package for Afghanistan. "We will continue to look for ways to provide more assistance for Afghans," Powell said, "including those farmers who have felt the impact of the [Taliban-imposed] ban on poppy cultivation." The new aid package, Powell continued, brought the year-to-date total U.S. aid to Afghanistan to more than $124 million, making the United States the world's largest donor to Afghanistan for the second year running.

Shelling out millions to acknowledged producers of opium, much of which finds its way to American streets, is itself a strategy of questionable wisdom. But even in the wake of [the] September 11th, [2001, terrorist attacks on America], with a war raging between the United States and Afghanistan and the blood of thousands of innocent American citizens quite possibly on the hands of the Afghan government, the foreign aid cornucopia continues to shower the Afghans with food and other forms of "humanitarian" aid purchased with dollars taken from U.S. taxpayers—the same taxpayers who are footing the bill for the war and the tens of billions of dollars' worth of devastation wrought by the terrorist attacks. On October 4th, 2001, President George W. Bush announced another aid package to Afghanistan and Afghan refugees in neighboring Central Asian republics. This latest gift, totaling $320 million, according to a fact sheet issued by the White House, brought the year-to-date total aid to Afghanistan to about $504 million.

Chapter 3

The Failure of Foreign Aid

The ongoing saga of U.S. aid to Afghanistan is but one episode in a long record of foreign aid waste and abuse. For decades, billions of taxpayer dollars have been sent overseas, allegedly for humanitarian causes. From massive military interventionism to bailouts of bankrupt Third World despots, Washington's budgetary priorities suggest that our leaders have been more concerned about the citizenry and governments of foreign nations than about their own:

• Over the years, our elected officials, Republican and Democrat alike, have dispatched military forces to the likes of Iraq, Somalia, and the Balkans to promote regional "stability"—yet decisive measures to close our own borders to a flood of illegal immigrants from Mexico and Central America have not been taken.

• Washington frets about building a national missile defense system, even in the wake of the September 11th attacks—but spends billions maintaining military bases overseas to protect allies like Japan and Germany.

• American foreign aid programs dole out vast sums to cash-strapped governments in Asia, Latin America, and Africa, to alleviate poverty and malnutrition—even as the federal government cuts off irrigation water to, and destroys the livelihoods of, thousands of farming families in the Klamath Basin of southern Oregon and northern California.

• Billions in taxpayer dollars go to assist Third World governments in building dams and modernizing energy-providing infrastructures, while America's once-promising nuclear-power industry is pushed to the brink of extinction by regulatory overkill.

• Much of the money taken from America's taxpayers is sent directly to regimes, like the Taliban, openly hostile to the U.S. Overall, taxpayer dollars have become America's number one export.

Despite its supposedly lofty ideals, foreign aid seldom if ever achieves its intended, or publicly stated, purposes. This is because foreign aid is not charity but international socialism. Hard-earned money is taken from U.S. taxpayers and redistributed abroad according to the whims of globalist micromanagers. It is viewed by its most doctrinaire supporters not just as a remedy for the suffering of the world's huddled masses, but as a just imposition on the greedy, exploitive, unfairly affluent societies of the West.

> *"Foreign aid seldom if ever achieves its intended, or publicly stated, purposes."*

In practice, like all socialist delusions, international wealth redistribution has precisely the opposite effect from that claimed. Instead of punishing the rich in America and elsewhere, foreign aid is yet another tax burden afflicting the middle class. The aid almost always goes directly to governments, not to individuals or private entities, and nearly always enriches and strengthens primarily the wealthy and the politically connected in recipient nations. They in turn use the funds to line their own pockets, build monuments to their own vanity, and enlarge their military, economic, and police-state capabilities. The suffering poor, meanwhile, continue to endure disease and poverty under the heel of their oppressors, with salvation always just a bailout away.

Roots of Foreign Aid

In the beginning, globalists understood that the American public would not accept an overt dole of tax monies to foreign governments. They therefore conceived the idea of using international currency manipulation as a cover for diverting public funds to overseas beneficiaries. In 1934, an obscure government agency known as the Exchange Stabilization Fund (ESF) was created to "stabilize" foreign currency exchange rates in the wake of President Franklin D. Roosevelt's unconstitutional confiscation of privately owned gold. Before long, the ESF began issuing "stabilization loans" to prop up bankrupt foreign governments, something it was neither constitutionally nor statutorily authorized to do. The first such loan, to the Mexican government in January 1936, was designed as a currency "exchange" between the United States and Mexican treasuries, for which Mexico paid interest in pesos on the resulting American account. From that day forward, the ESF has quietly but steadily enlarged its authority to issue bailout loans to anemic Third World economies. Because the secretary of the treasury enjoys the sole discretionary power to authorize ESF financial activities, Congress, according to researcher Anna Schwarz, "has ceded to the executive branch the power to extend foreign aid without prior congressional approval."

In 1995, the infamous Mexican bailout abruptly brought the ESF's activities to public attention. After Congress firmly rejected the White House's demand for funding, the Clinton administration created widespread outrage by handing Mexico $12 billion in ESF funds, by far the largest amount of aid the ESF had ever given. Yet despite the bad publicity, the ESF continues to ply its dubious trade. In 1997–98, for example, it was a major contributor to the international bailout of the stricken economies of East Asia.

Better known than the ESF is the International Monetary Fund (IMF), which was founded in 1946 as part of the Bretton Woods Act. Its architects were socialist economist John Maynard Keynes and Assistant Secretary to the U.S. Treasury Harry Dexter White, a Soviet spy. Stabilization of foreign exchange rates was the IMF's stated purpose. But like the ESF, the IMF soon began expanding its range of activities to include bailout loans to bankrupt regimes.

In the wake of World War II, government-subsidized international compassion was an easy sell. But White, a subversive with a subtle mind for international finance, was well aware that the IMF had a purpose very different from its alleged humanitarian goals. In early drafts of his IMF proposal, White urged that the IMF "pierce at the weakest points . . . extreme nationalism" and that "a breach must be made and widened in the outmoded and disastrous economic policy of each-country-for-itself-and-the-devil-take-the-weakest." As White's notes imply and its subsequent history shows, the IMF is meant to act as an international economic leveller, siphoning money from the citizens of "unjustly" wealthy nations and redistributing it among the political classes of poor countries. The IMF is also intended to be an instrument for attacking economic sovereignty by wresting fiscal autonomy from debtor nations in return for keeping the money spigots open.

IMF loans are typically issued at well below market interest rates, at attractive terms of payment, and are thus a powerful inducement for fiscally irresponsible regimes to go on the international dole. But there is a price to pay for U.S.-backed IMF largesse. Associated with such loans are terms of "conditionality" that usually undermine the financial sovereignty of the debtor and further socialize the economy. Borrowers are often required to raise revenue through tax hikes, to reform and enlarge the government regulatory apparatus, to restrict imports, and to submit to periodic international inspection and review of government policies. Such statist measures both dilute national sovereignty—as White originally intended—and dampen economic performance, ensuring that the country in question will continue to require international assistance to stay afloat. In a recent article in *The New Republic*, economist Joseph Stiglitz described the IMF's modus operandi:

> The IMF likes to go about its business without outsiders asking too many questions. In theory, the fund supports democratic institutions in the nations it assists. In practice, it undermines the democratic process by imposing policies. Officially, of course, the IMF doesn't "impose" anything. It "negotiates" the conditions for receiving aid. But all the power in the negotiations is on one side—the IMF's—and the fund rarely allows sufficient time for consensus-building or even widespread consultations with either parliaments or civil society. Sometimes the IMF dispenses with the pretense of openness altogether and negotiates secret covenants. When the IMF decides to assist a country, it dispatches a "mission" of economists. These economists frequently lack extensive experience in the country. . . . They work hard, poring over numbers deep into the night. But their task is impossible. In a period of days or, at most, weeks, they are charged with developing a coherent program sensitive to the needs of the country. Needless to say, a little number-crunching rarely provides adequate insights into the development strategy for an entire nation.

The modern IMF derives revenue from several sources. Its reserves are expressed in terms of SDRs, or "Special Drawing Rights," which are officially derived from a basket of weighted major currencies. IMF members are required to pay a "subscription quota" whose amount is determined by the IMF on the basis of its perceived economic position relative to the rest of the world. The pool of quota subscriptions is the IMF's primary source of revenue, amounting to more than $270 billion. Of this total amount, the United States, predictably, pays the lion's share, a sum of roughly $48 billion. In addition, the IMF has an emergency borrowing pool for expedited bailouts known aptly as NABs (New Arrangements to Borrow). The total amount of NAB funds available is roughly $44 billion, of which the United States accounts for about one-fifth, or $8.7 billion.

The IMF also spent several decades quietly stockpiling gold, which according to the original Articles of Agreement was required as a percentage of subscriptions and for payment of membership charges. Thus, during the decades when the U.S. government forbade its own citizens to invest in gold, and worked ceaselessly to rid the world of precious metal currency standards, the IMF was confiscating gold from member countries, including the United States. The IMF closed its own "gold window" in 1978—but not before it had accumulated gold reserves worth about $7.5 billion, which it continues to hold "for prudential reasons [and] to meet unforeseen contingencies," according to an IMF fact sheet.

Also created as part of the Bretton Woods agreement was the World Bank, a labyrinth of regional lending banks, a dispute settlement agency, a finance corporation, a pair of global development funds, and various subsidiary organizations. Like the IMF, the World Bank specializes in loans below market terms. As with the IMF, the United States financial commitment to the World Bank is enormous. Our capital stock in the World Bank's International Finance Corporation (IFC), for example, was more than $569 million as of June 2000, or more than one-fourth of the total of $2.3 billion.

Unilateral Aid

The foreign aid racket, though, is not confined to the machinations of multilateral vehicles like the IMF and the World Bank. The U.S. taxpayer also pays for billions of dollars of unilateral aid administered directly by the United States Agency for International Development (USAID) to every conceivable species of deadbeat regime. President John F. Kennedy, who set up USAID in 1961, said at the time that:

> there is no escaping our obligations: our moral obligations as a wise leader in the interdependent community of free nations—our economic obligations as the wealthiest people in a world of largely poor people. . . . To fail to meet those obligations now would be disastrous; and, in the long run, more expensive. For widespread poverty and chaos lead to a collapse of existing political and social structures which would inevitably invite the advance of totalitarianism into every weak and unstable area.

Yet 40 years later, those areas of the world most dependent on USAID and other sources of foreign aid are generally worse off than ever, relative to the rest of the world. As USAID administrator Andrew Natsios recently lamented, "we have been losing the war against hunger in sub-Saharan Africa. . . . [I]n Africa, [estimates] indicate that the number of hungry . . . will increase by about 10 million a year over the next decade." This, despite the countless billions in foreign aid that have poured into Africa decade after decade.

The situation is the same in South Asia, especially India, which has been the world's number one recipient of foreign aid since the '60s, yet has fallen further and further behind the rest of the world in development. Even as countries in East and Southeast Asia modernize, South Asia remains a tragic sinkhole of war, disease, and poverty unmatched anywhere else in the world.

Then there are the permanent international welfare-roll states of Latin America, utterly and inextricably dependent on foreign aid in its various forms. When this writer lived in Argentina in the late '70s, that country had a semi-modern, unstable economy with a crippling load of international debt. Inflation was so high that Argentines could not generally save money at all, but had to protect their wealth by buying land and converting it to more stable currencies. More than 20 years later, Argentina's debt is higher still, and her inflation rate has investors and savers alike scurrying to convert evaporating pesos into dollars and more stable investment mediums. Much the same could be said of Brazil, Mexico, and most of the rest of Latin America.

Despite all the financial and political turmoil in the Third World, American investors continue to move their business outside U.S. borders, to the low-cost labor markets of Latin America, Asia, and, to a smaller degree, Africa. This is partly because America's regulatory climate has caused the costs of doing business at home to skyrocket. But more importantly, American corporations that move their operations and jobs abroad are shielded by taxpayer dollars from the consequences of risky overseas investments.

The Overseas Private Investment Corporation, or OPIC, was created at the same time as USAID, to use taxpayer dollars to protect multinational corporations from investment risk overseas. In conjunction with the availability of IMF and World Bank bailouts, OPIC helps to artificially protect overseas investors from shouldering investment risk in what would otherwise be unstable political and economic climates. Wealthy American multinational corporations may be secure in the knowledge that their investments are insured by taxpayer funds, and that high-risk economies where they market their products will stay open for business—courtesy of money "loaned" to risky regimes by the U.S. government.

Aid and Comfort

Foreign aid was instrumental in supporting many of the Communist regimes arrayed against the United States and her allies, including Ceaucescu's Romania and the former Soviet Union itself. Foreign aid demonstrably abetted and reinforced African dictatorships like Zaire's Mobutu and Ethiopia's Mengistu. And of course, the spigots have been open for the benefit of Afghanistan's Taliban.

American foreign aid continues to prop up the economies of America's two major foes, Russia and Communist China. In the case of the latter, the U.S. president has renewed China's Most-Favored Nation trading status year after year, permitting that Communist regime to flood American markets with cheap goods manufactured by slave laborers in the *Laogai* system. We shell out millions of dollars to China for development, and turn a blind eye to China's occupation of Tibet, its open threats to invade Taiwan, its programs of forced abortion and religious persecution, and other totalitarian practices. "For far too long the American people have been forced to subsidize the communist Chinese, under the false guise of free trade," fumed Congressman Ron Paul (R-Texas) recently. "Free trade is allowing individuals to exchange goods and services, not forcing Americans to subsidize with their involuntary tax dollars a brutal regime that runs completely contrary to our system of government, and has apparently been working to actually subvert our laws and our institutions." Aside from the Taliban, nowhere more than in China are we so clearly subsidizing an enemy of the United States, yet large numbers of Americans seem to accept reassurances that our "investments" in China will somehow redound to our long-term benefit.

Misconceptions

The widespread perception persists among Americans, encouraged by internationalists in both major parties, that foreign aid is essentially benign, despite its dismal track record of promoting poverty, strengthening dictatorships, and benefiting the rich and well-connected at the expense of America's middle class. Foreign aid still has vigorous defenders in Congress, among corporations that do business overseas, and in what journalist Graham Hancock termed the "aristocracy of mercy," the UN-dominated network of international aid agencies.

Internationalist apologists often claim that foreign aid, at around 1 percent of the national budget, is fiscally inconsequential and not worth the hype and rhetoric of its opponents. But this figure neglects the tens of billions of dollars of foreign aid laundered via the IMF and the World Bank. It also ignores legions of other government projects that certainly fall under the rubric of foreign aid, but are usually reckoned as something different, for budgetary or political purposes. Who can accurately compute the full cost of America's annual overseas military commitments, our OPIC guarantees to overseas investors, our preferential trade policies encouraging unfair foreign competition against American business, and the cost of defending the United States against foreign perils like Communism, which were built up in large measure by American dollars and technology transfers in the first place?

But even if government-administered foreign aid worked as advertised, Congress is nowhere authorized by the Constitution to send U.S. taxpayers' money overseas, however benevolent the reason.

Government-sponsored foreign aid must be terminated. When America's middleclass taxpaying public demands of Congress an end to government foreign aid in all its corrosive, insidious forms, the world's deserving poor will be better off. The tax burden on America's beleaguered middle class will be lightened. Most importantly, freedom will proliferate more decisively across the world as corrupt governments are forced to account for their profligacy, and American national sovereignty is reasserted.

Debt Relief Will Not Help Developing Nations Overcome Poverty

by William Easterly

About the author: *William Easterly is senior advisor in the Development Research Group at the World Bank and author of* The Elusive Quest for Growth: Economists' Misadventures in the Tropics.

Debt relief has become the feel-good economic policy of the new millennium, trumpeted by Irish rock star Bono, Pope John Paul II, and virtually everyone in between. But despite its overwhelming popularity among policymakers and the public, debt relief is a bad deal for the world's poor. By transferring scarce resources to corrupt governments with proven track records of misusing aid, debt forgiveness might only aggravate poverty among the world's most vulnerable populations.

Good Intentions

"Jubilee 2000 Sparked the Debt Relief Movement." No. Sorry, Bono, but debt relief is not new. As long ago as 1967, the U.N. Conference on Trade and Development argued that debt service payments in many poor nations had reached "critical situations." A decade later, official bilateral creditors wrote off $6 billion in debt to 45 poor countries. In 1984, a World Bank report on Africa suggested that financial support packages for countries in the region should include "multiyear debt relief and longer grace periods." Since 1987, successive G-7 [among Canada, France, Germany, Italy, Japan, the United Kingdom, and the United States] summits have offered increasingly lenient terms, such as postponement of repayment deadlines, on debts owed by poor countries. (Ironically, each new batch of terms and conditions was named after the opulent site of the G-7 meeting, such as the "Venice terms," the "Toronto terms," and the "London terms.") In the late 1980s and 1990s, the World Bank and International Monetary Fund (IMF) began offering special loan programs to African nations, es-

sentially allowing governments to pay back high-interest loans with low-interest loans—just as real a form of debt relief as partial forgiveness of the loans. The World Bank and IMF's more recent and well-publicized Highly Indebted Poor Countries (HIPC) debt relief program therefore represents but a deepening of earlier efforts to reduce the debt burdens of the world's poorest nations. Remarkably, the HIPC nations kept borrowing enough new funds in the 1980s and 1990s to more than offset the past debt relief: From 1989 to 1997, debt forgiveness for the 41 nations now designated as HIPCs reached $33 billion, while new borrowing for the same countries totaled $41 billion.

So by the time the Jubilee 2000 movement began spreading its debt relief gospel in the late 1990s, a wide constituency for alleviating poor nations' debt already existed. However, Jubilee 2000 and other pro-debt relief groups succeeded in raising the visibility and popularity of the issue to unprecedented heights. High-profile endorsements range from Irish rock star Bono to Pope John Paul II and the Dalai Lama to Harvard economist Jeffrey Sachs; even retiring U.S. Senator Jesse Helms has climbed onto the debt relief bandwagon. In that respect, Jubilee 2000 (rechristened "Drop the Debt" before the organization's campaign officially ended on July 31, 2001) should be commended for putting the world's poor on the agenda—at a time when most people in rich nations simply don't care—even if the organization's proselytizing efforts inevitably oversimplify the problems of foreign debt.

"Third World Debts Are Illegitimate." Unhelpful idea. Supporters of debt relief programs have often argued that new democratic governments in poor nations should not be forced to honor the debts that were incurred and mismanaged long ago by their corrupt and dictatorial predecessors. Certainly, some justice would be served if a legitimate and reformist new government refused to repay creditors foolish enough to have lent to a rotten old autocracy. But, in reality, there are few clear-cut political breaks with a corrupt past. The political factors that make governments corrupt tend to persist over time. How "clean" must the new government be to represent a complete departure from the misdeeds of an earlier regime? Consider President Yoweri Museveni of Uganda, about the strongest possible example of a change from the past—in his case, the notorious past of Ugandan strongman Idi Amin. Yet even Museveni's government continues to spend money on questionable military adventures in the Democratic Republic of the Congo. Would Mu-

> *"Debt relief is a bad deal for the world's poor."*

seveni qualify for debt relief under the "good new government" principle? And suppose a long-time corrupt politician remains in power, such as Kenyan President Daniel Arap Moi. True justice would instead call for such leaders to pay back some of their loot to development agencies, who could then lend the money to a government with cleaner hands—a highly unlikely scenario.

Making debt forgiveness contingent on the supposed "illegitimacy" of the original borrower simply creates perverse incentives by directing scarce aid resources to countries that have best proved their capacity to mismanage such funds. For example, Ivory Coast built not just one but two new national capitals in the hometowns of the country's previous rulers as it was piling up debt. Then it had a military coup and a tainted election. Is that the environment in which aid will be well used? Meanwhile, poor nations that did not mismanage their aid loans so badly—

"Poor people don't owe foreign debt—their governments do."

such as India and Bangladesh—now do not qualify for debt relief, even though their governments would likely put fresh aid resources to much better use.

Finally, the legitimacy rationale raises serious reputation concerns in the world's financial markets. Few private lenders will wish to provide fresh financing to a country if they know that a successor government has the right to repudiate the earlier debt as illegitimate. For the legitimacy argument to be at all convincing, the countries in question must show a huge and permanent change from the corruption of past regimes. Indeed, strict application of such a standard introduces the dread specter of "conditionality," i.e., the imposition of burdensome policy requirements on developing nations in exchange for assistance from international financial institutions. Only rather than focusing solely on economic policy conditions, the international lending agencies granting debt relief would now be compelled to make increasingly subjective judgments regarding a country's politics, governance structures, and adherence to the rule of law.

Debt Relief and Development

"Crushing Debts Worsen Third World Poverty." Wrong in more ways than one. Yes, the total long-term debt of the 41 HIPC nations grew from $47 billion in 1980 to $159 billion in 1990 to $169 billion in 1999, but in reality the foreign debt of poor countries has always been partly fictional. Whenever debt service became too onerous, the poor nations simply received new loans to repay old ones. Recent studies have found that new World Bank adjustment loans to poor countries in the 1980s and 1990s increased in lock step with mounting debt service. Likewise, another study found that official lenders tend to match increases in the payment obligations of highly indebted African countries with an increase in new loans. Indeed, over the past two decades, new lending to African countries more than covered debt service payments on old loans.

Second, debt relief advocates should remember that poor people don't owe foreign debt—their governments do. Poor nations suffer poverty not because of high debt burdens but because spendthrift governments constantly seek to redistribute the existing economic pie to privileged political elites rather than try to make the pie grow larger through sound economic policies. The debt-burdened government of Kenya managed to find enough money to reward President Moi's home region with the Eldoret International Airport in 1996, a facility that almost nobody uses.

Left to themselves, bad governments are likely to engage in new borrowing to replace the forgiven loans, so the debt burden wouldn't fall in the end anyway. And even if irresponsible governments do not run up new debts, they could always finance their redistributive ways by running down government assets (like oil and minerals), leaving future generations condemned to the same overall debt burden. Ultimately, debt relief will only help reduce debt burdens if government policies make a true shift away from redistributive politics and toward a focus on economic development.

"Debt Relief Allows Poor Nations to Spend More on Health and Education." No. In 1999, Jubilee 2000 enthused that with debt relief "the year 2000 could signal the beginning of dramatic improvements in healthcare, education, employment and development for countries crippled by debt." Unfortunately, such statements fail to recognize some harsh realities about government spending.

First, the iron law of public finance states that money is fungible: Debt relief goes into the same government account that rains money on good and bad uses alike. Debt relief enables governments to spend more on weapons, for example. Debt relief clients such as Angola, Ethiopia, and Rwanda all have heavy military spending (although some are promising to make cuts). To assess whether debt relief increases health and education spending, one must ask what such spending would have been in the absence of debt relief—a difficult question. However, if governments didn't spend the original loans on helping the poor, it's a stretch to expect them to devote new fiscal resources toward helping the poor.

Second, such claims assume that the central government knows where its money is going. A recent IMF and World Bank study found that only two out of 25 debt relief recipients will have satisfactory capacity to track where government spending goes within a year. At the national level, an additional study found that only 13 percent of central government grants for nonsalary education spending in Uganda (another recipient of debt relief) actually made it to the local schools that were the intended beneficiaries.

Finally, the very idea that the proceeds of debt relief should be spent on health and education contains a logical flaw. If debt relief proceeds are spent on social programs rather than used to pay down the debt, then the debt burden will remain just as crushing as it was before. A government can't use the same money twice—first to pay down foreign debt and second to expand health and education services for the poor. This magic could only work if health and education spending boosted economic growth and thus generated future tax revenues to service the debt. Unfortunately, there is little evidence that higher health and education spending is associated with faster economic growth.

> *"It would be hard to ensure that debt relief will truly benefit the poor unless there are conditions on the debt relief package."*

Conditional Debt Relief

"Debt Relief Will Empower Poor Countries to Make Their Own Choices." Not really. Pro-debt relief advocacy groups face a paradox: On one hand, they want debt relief to reach the poor; on the other, they don't want rich nations telling poor countries what to do. "For debt relief to work, let the conditions be set by civil society in our countries, not by big world institutions using it as a political tool," argued Kennedy Tumutegyereize of the Uganda Debt Network. Unfortunately, debt relief advocates can't have it both ways. Civil society remains weak in most highly indebted poor countries, so it would be hard to ensure that debt relief will truly benefit the poor unless there are conditions on the debt relief package.

Attempting to square this circle, the World Bank and IMF have made a lot of noise about consulting civil society while at the same time dictating incredibly detailed conditions on debt relief. The result is unlikely to please anyone. Debt relief under the World Bank and IMF's current HIPC initiative, for example, requires that countries prepare Poverty Reduction Strategy Papers. The World Bank's online handbook advising countries on how to prepare such documents runs well over 1,000 pages and covers such varied topics as macro-economics, gender, the environment, water management, mining, and information technology. It would be hard for even the most skilled policymakers in the advanced economies to follow such complex (no matter how salutary) advice, much less a government in a poor country suffering from scarcity of qualified managers. In reality, this morass of requirements emerged as the multilateral financial institutions sought to hit on all the politically correct themes while at the same time trying hard to make the money reach the poor. If the conditions don't work—and of course they won't—the World Bank and IMF can simply fault the countries for not following their advice.

"Debt Relief Hurts Big Banks." Wrong. During the 1970s and early 1980s, large commercial banks and official creditors based in rich nations provided substantial loans at market interest rates to countries such as Ivory Coast and Kenya. However, they pulled out of these markets in the second half of the 1980s and throughout the 1990s. In fact, from 1988 to 1997, such lenders received more in payments on old loans than they disbursed in new lending to high-debt poor countries. The multilateral development banks and bilateral lenders took their place, offering low-interest credit to poor nations. It's easy to understand why the commercial and official creditors pulled out. Not only did domestic economic mismanagement make high-debt poor countries less attractive candidates for potential loans, but with debt relief proposals in the air as early as 1979, few creditors wished to risk new lending under the threat that multilateral agencies would later decree loan forgiveness.

The IMF and World Bank announced the HIPC initiative of partial and conditional forgiveness of multilateral loans for 41 poor countries in September

1996. By the time the debt relief actually reached the HIPCs in the late 1990s, the commercial banks and high-interest official creditors were long gone and what was being forgiven were mainly "concessional" loans—i.e., loans with subsidized interest rates and long repayment periods. So really, debt relief takes money away from the international lending community that makes concessional loans to the poorest nations, potentially hurting other equally poor but not highly indebted nations if foreign aid resources are finite (as, of course, they are). Indeed, a large share of the world's poor live in India and China. Neither nation, however, is eligible for debt relief.

> *"Debt relief encourages borrowers to take on an excessive amount of new loans expecting that they too will be forgiven."*

"Debt Relief Boosts Foreign Investment in Poor Nations." A leap of faith. It is true that forgiving old debt makes the borrowers more able to service new debt, which in theory could make them attractive to lenders. Nevertheless, the commercial and official lenders who offer financing at market interest rates will not want to come back to most HIPCs any time soon. These lenders understand all too well the principle of moral hazard: Debt relief encourages borrowers to take on an excessive amount of new loans expecting that they too will be forgiven. Commercial banks obviously don't want to get caught with forgiven loans. And even the most charitable official lenders don't want to sign their own death warrants by getting stuck with forgiven debt. Both commercial and official lenders may want to redirect their resources to safer countries where debt relief is not on the table. Indeed, in 1991, the 47 least developed countries took in 5 percent of the total foreign direct investment (FDI) that flowed to the developing world; by 2000 their portion had dropped to only 2.5 percent. (Over the same period, the portion of global FDI captured by all developing nations dropped as well, from 22.3 to 15.9 percent.) Even capital flows to now lightly indebted "safe" countries might suffer from the perception that their debts also may be forgiven at some point. Ultimately, only the arms of multilateral development banks that provide soft loans—with little or no interest and very long repayment periods—are going to keep lending to HIPCs, and only then under very stringent conditions.

Economic Reform Cannot Be Imposed from the Outside

"Debt Relief Will Promote Economic Reform." Don't hold your breath. During the last two decades, the multilateral financial institutions granted "structural adjustment" loans to developing nations, with the understanding that governments in poor countries would cut their fiscal deficits and enact reforms—including privatization of state-owned enterprises and trade liberalization—that would promote economic growth. The World Bank and IMF made 1,055 separate adjustment loans to 119 poor countries from 1980 to 1999. Had such lend-

ing succeeded, poor countries would have experienced more rapid growth, which in turn would have permitted them to service their foreign debts more easily. Thirty-six poor countries received 10 or more adjustment loans in the 1980s and 1990s, and their average percentage growth of per capita income during those two decades was a grand total of zero. Moreover, such loans failed to produce meaningful reforms, and developing countries now cite this failure as justification for debt relief. Yet why should anyone expect that conditions on debt forgiveness would be any more effective in changing government policies and behavior than conditions on the original loans?

Partial and conditional debt forgiveness is a fait accompli. Expanding it to full and unconditional debt forgiveness—as some groups now advocate—would simply transfer more resources from poor countries that have used aid effectively to those that have wasted it in the past. The challenge for civil society, the World Bank, IMF, and other agencies is to ensure that conditional debt forgiveness really does lead to government reforms that enhance the prospects of poor countries.

How can we promote economic reform in the poorest nations without repeating past failures? The lesson of structural adjustment programs is that reforms imposed from the outside don't change behavior. Indeed, they only succeed in creating an easy scapegoat: Insincere governments can simply blame their woes on the World Bank and IMF's "harsh" adjustment programs while not doing anything to fundamentally change economic incentives and ignite economic growth. It would be better for the international financial institutions to simply offer advice to governments that ask for it and wait for individual countries to come forward with homegrown reform programs, financing only the most promising ones and disengaging from the rest. This approach has worked in promoting economic reform in countries such as China, India, and Uganda. Rushing through debt forgiveness and imposing complex reforms from the outside is as doomed to failure as earlier rounds of debt relief and adjustment loans.

The United States Should Not Support Family Planning Services in Developing Nations

by Laura L. Garcia

About the author: *Laura L. Garcia is a professor of philosophy at Boston College.*

We are faced with two facts: globalization is here to stay and its effects on the family have been largely negative. I wish to focus on the ways in which a particular ideology regarding human nature and human rights tends to undermine the family, even in its efforts to help. A more accurate understanding of the foundation of human rights and the human good can, in principle, redirect current efforts at social control in ways that are more family-friendly and that better preserve human dignity. I focus here especially on policies aimed at reducing population growth in developing countries and the number of pregnancies among unmarried women in every country, since these efforts have been zealously applauded in UN conferences and all but forced onto countries that wish to receive financial assistance from international agencies.

Current Population Control Strategies

Population controllers claim that overpopulation impedes economic development by perpetuating poverty and straining scarce resources. Skeptics claim that the threat of overwhelming population growth is a myth, but an inquiry into this issue is beyond the scope of this article. Since population growth in many Western nations barely reaches replacement levels, fears of overpopulation focus primarily on Third World nations and what can be done to influence their growth rates. The target of these efforts, of course, is women of childbearing age, with the fertility of these women seen as a threat to themselves, the economic growth of their countries, and the global environment. The first of these claims, that women's fertility is a threat to themselves and to their self-realization, links population-control efforts with the radical feminist ideology that has come to dominate the academy and the media in most Western nations, producing a powerful coalition of (we assume) well-intentioned but extremely determined social engineers.

This explains the many links between agencies of the United Nations and the population controllers, as illustrated in the choice of Dr. Fred Sai of Ghana to head the UN International Conference on Population and Development (Cairo, 1994). Sai is president of the International Planned Parenthood Federation. In his closing remarks in Cairo he claimed that "women are crippled by their own unbridled fertility." Secretary-general of the Beijing Conference on Women in 1995 was Gertrude Mangella of Tanzania, who is associated with the UN-recognized nongovernmental organization (NGO) Women's Environment and Development Organization (WEDO), cofounded by the well-known radical feminist Bella Abzug. For many years, feminists have urged the view that women have the same human rights as men (so far, so good), that this equality of human rights requires sameness of social roles (not so obvious), that this sameness can be achieved only by removing the differences between men and women with respect to childbearing and child rearing (to whatever extent possible), and that this requires control over women's fertility. Naturally, this "control" is not meant primarily to enable couples to conceive children or to allow them to decide the size of their own families, but to limit severely the number of children conceived by any woman—married or unmarried. The prevailing view is that this is best achieved by access to methods of sterilization (temporary or permanent) and to abortion whenever such methods fail to prevent an unwanted, or simply unintended, pregnancy.

This part of the feminist agenda, which fits comfortably with population control efforts, has been funded with a vengeance through both public and private international agencies. For example, the U.S. government allocated $410 million for international population control in fiscal year 1997. Further goals of radical feminism are tied more to the interests of economic globalization than to population control efforts per se, but the two ideologies nicely reinforce one another. In the interests of producing a supposed ideal of "equality" between men and women (an equality

> *"The U.S. government allocated $410 million for international population control in fiscal year 1997."*

that denies any significant differences between the two), men are to be coerced (or perhaps simply "reeducated") into assuming roles with respect to home and children exactly similar to those that women have generally performed, so that both can spend much of their time as productive participants in the workplace. People who tend to interfere with this ideal of fulfillment through career and prosperity, such as children or elderly parents, are to be cared for by privately or publicly funded institutions of various kinds. This vision of the utopian ideal means that adult women will spend a good deal of their time in the workforce and in training programs of various kinds, with less time to devote to children, and hence will increasingly resemble the typical Western career woman.

The drive to make contraceptives and abortion accessible to every woman (and even to girls) can be fueled by altruistic motives, seen as a way of helping women and the human race generally into a more enlightened future. Questions linger

> *"Some of the population control programs are clearly driven by . . . subtle (or not-so-subtle) forms of racism."*

over whether this agenda is truly in the interests of women, especially women in cultures less fragmented than in the West. As Elizabeth Fox-Genovese points out in her recent book *Feminism Is Not the Story of My Life*, many women find fulfillment and joy in their roles as mothers and homemakers, and they would appreciate the option to exercise these roles without the kinds of social and financial penalties that currently accompany them. "When motherhood is demoted from the center of women's lives to a parenthesis, children are demoted as well," she says. Setting these concerns aside, however, there is also room in the population control movement for less benign motives, and there are several indications that these are behind many programs promoting contraception and abortion, particularly in developing nations.

The Dark Side of Family Planning Policies

First, drug companies profit mightily from the worldwide marketing of contraceptives, from condoms to Norplant and "morning after" pills. There is a good deal of money to be made in the abortion business as well. Clinics do not provide these "services" free of charge, after all. One would expect that anyone having a genuine concern for the health and welfare of women would respond to the expressed needs of women themselves, but not so. Leanardo Casco of Honduras complains that "in our hospitals and in our health-care system, we have a lot of problems getting basic medicines—things like penicillin and antibiotics. There is a terrible shortage of basic medicines, but you can find the cabinets full of condoms, pills, and IUDs." Since 1969, the U.S. Agency for International Development has spent more money on population control programs than on other health programs. In some years, it spent three times more on contraceptive "reeducation" than on health care.

Second, some of the population control programs are clearly driven by eugenics boosters of various kinds and by subtle (or not-so-subtle) forms of racism. In a recent book promoting cloning as a preferred form of reproduction (think of how it enhances control!), Dr. Gregory Pence tries to allay fears that this might eliminate old-fashioned methods of reproduction by opining that "for every high-minded couple who produces a superior child by NST [nuclear somatic transfer, i.e., cloning] there would be a Brazilian couple who produces nine children by normal sex." (An ethicist at Rutgers University has noticed the bald bigotry evidenced here, where North American couples are birthing better babies through modern technologies while Latinos are still rutting away, turning out their litters of "inferiors.")

The real irony is that, regardless of their intent, current methods of population control that rely heavily on contraception and abortion do little to reduce out-of-wedlock pregnancies and often serve to exacerbate some of the very problems they are supposed to relieve. One assumption of the sexual revolution that has become cemented in the minds of many is that participating in the all-you-can-eat sexual buffet should be cost free, at least in principle. Contraceptives and abortion would remove the possibility of an unwanted child and of any health problems (especially sexually transmitted diseases, including AIDS). The facts do little to support this assumption, however. Condoms are notoriously ineffective in preventing pregnancy, so the promotion of condoms for this purpose, especially among teenagers, both sends the message that their sexual activity is expected (and to some extent accepted) and encourages a false sense of security. The track record of condoms in preventing AIDS and other STDs is even worse, so that "safe sex" is usually far from it.

A brief glance at the statistics from the United States in the period from 1960 to the present, when contraception and abortion have been heavily promoted, shows skyrocketing rates of out-of-wedlock pregnancies and abortions, though both rates have declined slightly in recent years. One indication that the "safe-sex" message is failing is that in the years 1988 to 1995, the nonmarital birthrate among sexually experienced teenage girls 15–19 years old (those who have ever had sex) rose almost 30 percent, even while the total birthrate in this group was dropping. The birthrate among sexually active girls (those who had sex in the past three months) rose 31 percent during this same period. So the 9 percent drop in birthrates cannot be explained by better use of contraceptives among teens. Nor can it be explained by the 33 percent increase in condom use during this period, since this is more than offset by a 45 percent decrease in the use of (far more effective) oral contraceptives. Further, while 80 percent of the teens surveyed said they had learned about STDs in school, most believed that condoms would protect them against any risk of STDs. They were completely unaware that condoms offer no protection against many of the most common STDs.

> *"[Abortion] continues to be promoted among developing countries as the final solution to their population and economic woes."*

One group of physicians behind the report on these statistics concludes that increased abstinence among teenagers is what explains the lower overall number of pregnancies and births. (The abortion rate did not increase during this period but instead dropped among girls aged 10–19 by over 28 percent between 1990 and 1995.) Since abstinence is the only truly effective way to prevent both pregnancy and STDs, it is disturbing that so little attention and funding have been given to abstinence education in our schools and in our efforts to promote responsible sexual behaviors at home and worldwide. . . .

The Wrongs of Abortion

Abortion is a terrible offense. No respect for the liberty or preferences of the mother or father of the child (or of other interested parties) can make this act acceptable. Concern for women faced with unwanted pregnancies could and should lead us instead to embrace a more inclusive compassion—promoting greater respect for women, encouraging teenage abstinence, and offering assistance through private and public agencies for women who choose adoption for their children or who are raising children in adverse circumstances.

The widespread practice of abortion, which in many Western nations is claiming a third of all children conceived, desensitizes us as a culture against other attacks on the vulnerable (the physically impaired, the elderly, the seriously ill). It drives wedges between men and women (who might well choose other options if the fathers were supportive of them), and between parents and children, who must wonder what will happen to them when they too become ill or inconvenient. Widespread and unrestricted access to abortion has not delivered on its promises. It has not reduced the number of unwanted pregnancies, it has not improved the relations between the sexes, it has not reduced the number of single-parent families. In every way, one could say that this particular experiment in living is a catastrophic failure. Yet it continues to be promoted among developing countries as the final solution to their population and economic woes.

It is hard to imagine that aggressive marketing of abortion in countries with social, moral, and religious objections to it can be based on anything other than a desire for greater profits for those who offer these "services" or a desire to reduce the numbers in poorer countries by any means necessary. The United Nations, for example, through its Population Fund, allocated $50 million to China in a five-year assistance program beginning in 1979, the year China instituted its coercive one-child policy. In 1983, when the fitting of IUDs in all Chinese women of childbearing age with one child became mandatory, a new IUD factory was built with the assistance of UNFPA (the United Nations Fund for Population Activities). Since 1979, this organization has given $157 million in aid to China, despite the UN's explicit commitment in its Declaration on Human Rights to the "basic right of all couples and individuals to decide freely and responsibly the number and spacing of their children." Given the sheer brutality of the Chinese policy and the horror tales surrounding its enforcement, the complicity of the United Nations in this abuse of women, children, and families is without excuse. Whatever the economic problems in China, it is impossible to justify this war against women and babies as a solution to them.

Given these objections to abortion, many would contend that a more aggressive campaign to encourage the use of contraceptives is the answer, so that fewer unintended pregnancies will occur, reducing the demand for abortion. This sounds reasonable, but the results have not materialized. With respect to teen pregnancies, for example, the evidence is that distributing contraceptives to young people confidentially and free of charge increases the likelihood that they will "experiment" with sex and does little to decrease their chances of pregnancy. Teenagers are notoriously irresponsible, after all; they will often use a barrier device improperly, forget to take an oral contraceptive pill, or perhaps fail to make use of either method out of a sense of guilt or fear of offending their "partner." One former abortion provider told an audience in Montana that she loved to go into high schools to promote the use of contraceptives, since if she could convince a girl to go on the pill, she could usually expect to see her in the clinic for an abortion within a few months' time.

> *"The millions of dollars that are wasted every year on misguided antipopulation programs could be better directed into programs that teach literacy."*

Finally, efforts to free women from child-related tasks and move them into the global marketplace often run roughshod over the values of the women involved. There is certainly no objection to providing women with the protections and opportunities consonant with their dignity as human persons. But the virtual insistence that women should desire a small family and a large salary denies many women the opportunity to set their own priorities in these matters. Removing women from the home in large numbers has hardly contributed to family stability in the West. Statistics in the United States show that the greatest incidence of violent crime and adolescent sexual activity takes place between the hours of 3:00 and 7:00 P.M., when both parents are away. The dominant form of feminism in the academy today fails to acknowledge two facts about raising children: it can be deeply engaging and rewarding, and it takes a lot of actual time (not just quality time) to do it properly. If women are doing the lion's share of this work, there should be ways of structuring society to enable them to realize their other noble ambitions as well and to encourage their participation in public life and in the workforce when they want or need to be there. But this should be done in such a way that it multiplies the options open to women, rather than eliminating the option to devote large portions of their time and energy to home and children. . . .

A Family-Friendly Population Policy

There are at least four ways in which the global economy, including its political and charitable involvements, can strengthen families and improve the lot of women with less cost and greater effectiveness than the programs currently offer:

1. Teach natural family planning (NFP) to young women and married couples. Current methods of natural family planning are effective and cost almost nothing. They treat a woman's fertility as a positive and important aspect of her humanity and work with her body's natural cycles to achieve or avoid a pregnancy. As a side benefit, this method promotes greater respect for women on the part of men and even on the part of women themselves. It leaves decisions about the number and spacing of children up to each couple, rather than imposing an alien ideal on them. Further, its use to avoid pregnancy requires some time of abstinence within each cycle, which is both an aid to developing important virtues of consideration and self-restraint and a further sign that the woman is not simply an object of use, even for her husband.

One argument against widespread reliance on natural family planning is that women will continue to be exploited by men and will sometimes engage in self-destructive sexual behavior themselves, and that NFP will not protect them in these instances. Addressing these problems means trying to bring it about that men are not allowed to exploit women and that men and women avoid irresponsible behaviors. Although this is more difficult to achieve than providing abortions and contraceptives, and certainly less profitable, it is still the place to attack the problem. What we have created instead is an environment in which women are expected to embrace the idea of cost-free sex, even while bemoaning the fact that men are unwilling to commit to permanent relationships.

2. Encourage abstinence among teenagers and others who are unmarried. This can be done in many ways, and there are now several programs teaching abstinence in the schools at every level, public or private. The U.S. Centers for Disease Control admits that the factor most responsible for the decrease in teen pregnancy and birth throughout the nineties is an increasing commitment to abstinence among teenagers, what they call "changing attitudes toward premarital sex.". . .

3. Provide literacy programs and genuinely liberal educations for women. The millions of dollars that are wasted every year on misguided antipopulation programs could be better directed into programs that teach literacy and provide educational options for both women and men. These funds could also be designated for more comprehensive health-care programs that would respond to the expressed needs

> *"Family planning has degenerated into quotas, and human beings have become targets."*

of local citizens rather than to the social agenda of an aggressive minority in economically powerful nations. Faced with the alarming rise in prostitution in many African countries, population controllers offer women condoms and abortion. Surely we could do better for these women by providing more immediate help in terms of food and housing, and by educational and job training programs that would enable them to earn a living in some other way. Strengthening marriage and family life would also lead to fewer abandoned and impoverished women, but this is clearly not on the agenda of the United Nations these days.

There is frightening inconsistency in a feminist ideology that seeks to "empower" women by encouraging them to wage war on their fertility and to see children as enemies of their success and fulfillment. First, this simply does not correspond to the way most women view their children, whom they see as gifts and as great sources of joy and hope for the future. Second, the self-proclaimed benefactors of women are not above turning reproductive "rights" into duties, ultimately closing off some choices in the name of offering a choice.

The cynical treatment of poor women as pawns in the population game shows the true colors of these programs' promoters. They are hardly pro-woman, and certainly not pro-choice. In India, a program of massive sterilizations for men and women and the distribution of thousands of IUDs (which are illegal in the United States due to dangerous side effects) resulted in hundreds of men dying from tetanus infections after vasectomies and a large percentage of women suffering from infections and punctured uteri from botched tubal ligations or IUD implants, since follow-up care was nonexistent. Many women were coerced or bribed into accepting sterilization, and then faced a procedure that averaged 45 seconds and left them lying side-by-side on a concrete floor moaning in pain. Ashish Bose, one of India's most prominent social scientists and a member of a government commission to study India's population problem, laments that "family planning has degenerated into quotas, and human beings have become targets."

4. Encourage the growth of market over centrally controlled economies. Here we have a worthy goal for which the tactics of the World Bank and USAID [the U.S. government agency responsible for sending aid to other nations] are appropriate, and where they could do enormous good for the human family. The noted scholar Julian Simon argues persuasively that the most important factor in the economic health of any nation is the basic structure of its economy, and that the effect of population growth is negligible or nonexistent. Since 1986, "the economics profession has turned almost completely away from the previous view that population growth is a crucial negative factor in economic development." For example, if we look at pairs of countries with the same culture and history and the same standard of living up until they split apart after World War II, such as North and South Korea, "the market-directed economies have performed much better than the centrally planned economies. . . . These data provide solid evidence that an enterprise system works better than a planned economy. This powerful explanation of economic development cuts the ground from under population growth as the likely explanation," says Simon.

In fact, population growth sometimes has a positive effect on economic development, in complete contradiction to the doomsday predictions of many environmentalists. When a given natural resource becomes scarce or more costly, people create more resources of all kinds, sometimes substituting artificial materials for natural ones. Scarcity is what drives innovation, invention, and new technologies.

As Simon sums up, "The general trend is toward natural resources becoming less and less important with economic development." If the international community is genuinely interested in improving the standard of living for all peoples they would do well to learn from this research and focus their efforts on encouraging economic reforms rather than attacking the human resources of developing countries. This is something they are well equipped to do. The opportunities abound at this very moment in countries that are turning away from centrally planned economies but have yet to establish secure free-market systems.

Family Planning and Human Rights

There are few signs that the global economy is interested in genuine service to the deeper aspirations of men and women, or that corporations and Western governments are willing to commit themselves to defending the dignity and basic freedoms of each human being. But as long as the rhetoric of human rights is still alive, in the United Nations and in public debates about these issues, there is hope that the true meaning of that phrase will eventually have its effect. Human rights are inviolable only if they are grounded in human nature, not in individual quirks or preferences. There are practical incentives to end the current aggressive population policies and replace them with initiatives that will promote economic development, further the cause of women, and give couples greater power over their procreative decisions without trampling on basic human rights and without removing the sovereignty of any nation. What we have tried so far has not accomplished its goals, creating instead a host of enemies and an even greater host of casualties. In this new millennium, surely some different strategies are in order.

Chapter 4

Can Democracy Succeed in Developing Nations?

Chapter Preface

Democratic governments such as the United States encourage the growth of democracy in developing nations because they believe in the political and ideological goals of democracy itself. But the United States also promotes democracy in the hope that it will lead to greater economic growth and political stability in the developing world. In the words of President George W. Bush, "by promoting democracy we lay the foundation for a better and more stable world."

However, promoting democracy in the developing world is something of a "chicken-and-the-egg" problem: Advocates of democracy believe it will strengthen stability and economic development in poor nations, but skeptics point out that democracy is most successful in nations that have already achieved economic and political stability.

David W. Yang, executive director of the Institute for Global Democracy, sums up the ways in which democracy can promote economic development and stability:

> While a democracy cannot ensure that economic policies will always be sound, it can provide a more productive environment for the saving and investment of domestic capital. It can do so because the democratic values of equality, transparency, and accountability translate in the economic sphere to clearly defined property and labor rights, free but well-regulated exchanges in the marketplace, just settlement of contract disputes, and fair taxation.

On the other hand, Adam Przeworski, Michael E. Alvarez, Jose Antonio Cheibub, and Fernando Limongi, authors of *Democracy and Development*, write that "any casual glance at the world will show that poor countries tend to have authoritarian regimes, and wealthy countries democratic ones. . . . Democracies are much more likely to survive in affluent societies." Democracies often fail in developing nations because widespread poverty contributes to political instability. Because democracy is a relatively fragile form of government, some developing nations may not be ready for democracy. Leaders such as former prime minister of Singapore Lee Kuan Yew have even used this line of reasoning to defend authoritarian regimes: "I do not believe that democracy necessarily leads to development. . . . What a country needs to develop is discipline more then democracy."

The question of whether economic prosperity must precede democratic government—or vice versa—is one of the issues considered by the authors in the following chapter as they examine the prospects for democracy in developing nations.

Democracy Can Succeed in Developing Nations

by Leon Aron

About the author: *Leon Aron is a resident scholar at the American Enterprise Institute, a Washington, D.C., think tank that promotes limited government, private enterprise, and a strong foreign policy and national defense.*

The post–cold war era has produced something new in world history: an abundance of poor democracies. There are now some seventy nations with a gross domestic product (GDP) below $10,000 per capita and with the basic attributes of democratic government. These regimes have been greeted in the West mostly with scorn and condescension. In reading about them, we learn of their economic struggles, their democratic deficiencies, their uncertain prospects. But their existence can also be seen as a hopeful sign, even a remarkable success story, and as a tribute to the universal appeal of freedom and self-government.

Until 1989, democracy was rare in "less developed nations." Stable democracy seemed to be a luxury only rich nations could afford, the icing on the cake of a five-digit per capita GDP. To be sure, the correlation was never perfect. An assortment of poor countries—India, the island nations of the English-speaking Caribbean, Venezuela—had been democracies for decades. Almost all the states of Central and South America had had democratic interludes sandwiched between periods of military dictatorship. And in the course of the 1980s, a few poor countries held breakthrough elections that launched durable democracies—notably El Salvador in 1982. But protodemocratic regimes that sprang up in the Third World tended to be torn apart by the magnetic tensions of the bipolar cold war circuit. Within a few years, most devolved into leftist or rightist dictatorships, often beset by guerrilla insurgencies.

Now all that has changed. While the end of the cold war did not in itself introduce democracy in poor nations, it greatly improved the odds for democratic stabilization. No longer assets in a global struggle, poor countries were left to their own devices—and many succeeded in establishing tenuous and flawed but real democracies, in Central and South America, Southeast Asia, and Africa, as well as in the former Soviet bloc.

These poor democracies are bare-bones democracies. They face real economic challenges, and their civic cultures are underdeveloped by the standards of the West. Yet, for all their conspicuous faults, they feature basic individual rights and political liberties. Their people enjoy freedom of speech, the right to petition government, freedom of assembly, and the freedom to travel abroad. The opposition can organize and participate in politics, criticize the government, distribute canvassing materials, and compete for local and national office in free and more or

> *"The story of the twenty-first century . . . could be greatly influenced by the evolution of the poor democracies."*

less fair elections, whose results, in the end, reflect the will of the majority. Finally, poor democracies have newspapers free of government censorship. These characteristics distinguish poor democracies both from nondemocracies (such as Burma, China, Cuba, North Korea, Saudi Arabia, Turkmenistan, and Vietnam) and from pseudodemocracies, regimes decked out in the institutional trappings of democracy, yet falling short on one or more of the criteria suggested above (for instance, Azerbaijan, Egypt, Kazakhstan, or Malaysia).

In economic terms, the poor democracies cover an enormous range: from Nigeria, Bangladesh, and India (with per capita GDPs of $440 or below, according to World Bank figures for 1999), to Peru, Russia, Jamaica, and Panama (between $2,000 and $3,000), to Poland, Chile, Hungary, and the Czech Republic (between $4,000 and $5,000), and, in the upper crust, Argentina ($7,555), South Korea ($8,500), Barbados ($8,600), Malta ($9,200), and Slovenia ($10,000). (For comparison, the rich democracies enjoy per capita GDPs over $20,000: Canada, Italy, and France are between $20,000 and $24,000; the United States is at $32,000; and Switzerland and Luxembourg are at $38,000 and $43,000. The intermediate category—democracies with per capita GDPs between $10,000 and $20,000—includes Portugal, Spain, Greece, and Israel.) Even excluding ministates and protectorates, poor democracies are now more numerous than regimes of any other type.

For most of the past century, history was shaped by the global struggle between democracy and totalitarianism, acted out by some of the world's largest industrial and military powers: the United States, Germany, Japan, Russia, and China. The story of the twenty-first century, by contrast, could be greatly influenced by the evolution of the poor democracies.

Different Roads to Democracy

The poor democracies and their wealthy cousins arrived at democratic institutions by very different paths. Beginning in the Middle Ages, the Western European road to democracy was paved with slow gains in rights and immunities, as nobles secured independence from the king and as towns, the church, universities, and corporations grew progressively freer from local lords. Over centuries, a system of mutual rights and obligations took shape in the feudal relations of vassalage. Gradually, customary arrangements acquired the force of law: the sanctity of contracts freely entered into; the impartiality of courts; the self-policing of corporations, guilds, and professional associations. Local self-government preceded national democracy by centuries.

In many respects, the poor democracies' experience has been the opposite. Here, the institutions, ethical norms, and practices of modernity failed to develop under the ancien regime. And if most poor democracies lack a democratic culture, the formerly communist nations are at a special disadvantage. Except in a few Central European nations such as Estonia and the Czech Republic, the "software" of liberal capitalist democracy either never existed or was badly eroded or even extirpated by decades of communism. It has been said that the postcommunist societies have had to start out as "democracies without democrats," for the totalitarian state systematically destroyed, corrupted, or subverted even nonpolitical voluntary associations, the very groupings that promote and help internalize self-restraint and compliance with rules—church, neighborhood, profession, and, at the height of Stalinism, family itself.

The revolt against the totalitarian or authoritarian state that gave birth to the poor democracies was, in most instances, a national rather than a local affair. A powerful national consensus formed in favor of personal

> *"Most of [the developing nations that have embraced democracy] were corrupt for centuries before they became democratic."*

and political liberty. This led to the embrace of the principles of democratic governance and the swift adoption of institutions through which they could be effected. Far from being an outgrowth of local self-government, democratization in these countries was an exercise in superimposing borrowed political structures—enthusiastically borrowed, to be sure—upon societies whose everyday social arrangements and values had been inherited largely intact from antidemocratic regimes.

Another crucial distinction between the poor democracies and their richer, more mature cousins lies in the relationship between property and political power. In Western Europe, the medieval unity of economic and political power eroded over centuries, until the economic and political spheres became largely (although never entirely) separate. In most poor democracies, this critical divergence is only beginning, haltingly, to take place. Political power translates into ownership or economic control, and vice versa, to the benefit of the elder, the tribal chief, the mayor, the governor, the kolkhoz chairman, or the factory manager.

Long experience of self-rule at the level of the town, the congregation, the guild, the local charity, together with the separation of the economic and political realms, forms the tallest hedge a culture can place against lawlessness and graft. One hesitates before stealing from a till one has freely voted to fill, or breaking rules one has freely agreed to uphold. The most immediate and conspicuous effect of the poor democracies' shortcut to political modernity has been corruption, which to a varying but very high degree plagues all of them.

Of course, even in the West, these formidable safeguards were no guarantee against the fraud and corruption of early capitalism.

> An impatience to be rich, a contempt for those slow but sure gains which are the proper reward of industry, patience, and thrift, spread through society . . . [and] took possession of the grave Senators of the City, . . . Deputies, Aldermen. It was [easy] and . . . lucrative to put forth a lying prospectus announcing a new stock, to persuade ignorant people that the dividends could not fall short of twenty percent. . . . Every day some new bubble was puffed into existence, rose buoyant, shone bright, burst and was forgotten.

This could have been written about any number of poor democracies. It is an excerpt from [historian Thomas Babington] Macaulay's description of London at the end of the seventeenth century, in the aftermath of the Glorious Revolution. For that matter, there remain well-publicized pockets of corruption in modern rich democracies: New York and Chicago through most of the past century, Marseilles or Palermo today.

But in the poor democracies, corruption is pervasive and systemic. It is a central issue in the national politics of Peru and Mexico, Colombia and Venezuela, Brazil and the Czech Republic, Bulgaria and Romania, all the countries of the former Soviet Union, the Philippines, Turkey, India, South Korea, Nigeria, and South Africa.

Most of these countries were corrupt for centuries before they became democratic (or capitalist). There is, furthermore, a matter of perception: Government bureaucrats under dictators, and party elites under communism, tended to steal and consume inconspicuously, certainly without media attention, while the new class that has succeeded them is far less secretive and is relentlessly pursued by the media. (Hence, perhaps, the American businessman's enthusiasm for nondemocratic China, where graft is centralized and strictly rank-rationed, workers are docile, secrets are protected by the police, and the lines of authority are etched by fear in the hearts of underlings, ensuring a bribe's effectiveness—by contrast with, say, Russia, a poor democracy where fear of government has been mostly forgotten, the media are brazen and hungry for scandal, prerogatives are hopelessly confused, and secrets have a half-life of two days.)

> *"In most poor democracies . . . democracy was the paramount societal goal, with capitalism a distant second item on the agenda."*

Where democracy arrived suddenly, state wealth, formerly appropriated by the dictator or the party and guarded with guns by the army and secret police, was delivered into the custody of a much less cohesive group of first-generation democratic politicians. The abolition of state ownership or control of the economy almost overnight turned state assets into a beached whale for vultures to feast on—with bureaucrats controlling access to the beach via quotas, licenses, and rigged auctions. Occurring in an institutional vacuum, privatization—whether in Mexico, Brazil, India, the Czech Republic, or Russia—necessarily brought together a newly empowered (often, newly legalized) and very hungry entrepreneur and an impoverished bureaucrat—with the predictable result.

Capitalism by Majority

Another defining attribute of poor democracies is their historically unprecedented combination of elections by universal suffrage with early, crude, and brutal capitalism, what Marx called the capitalism of "primary accumulation."

In the West, capitalism preceded universal suffrage by at least a century. In most poor democracies, certainly those of the postcommunist variety, democracy was the paramount societal goal, with capitalism a distant second item on the agenda. (In some countries, we have been treated to the sight, never before beheld, of modern democracy essentially without capitalism—for example, in Ukraine between 1991 and 1995.) This has produced a novel socioeconomic organism: capitalism whose key elements require approval by the voters, elements as basic as private ownership of large industrial enterprises, the right to buy and sell land, to hire and fire workers, and market prices for rent and utilities.

"Poor democracies have had to start out with backward, autarkic, often militarized state-owned economics."

Where the foundations of modern capitalism are being laid for the first time in countries governed by majority rule, the consequences for both capitalism and democracy are profound. The experience of the poor democracies is a reminder of the fundamental heterogeneity of capitalism and democracy: The former institutionalizes inequality, while the latter institutionalizes equality. Amalgamated in the West by the weight of time and custom, capitalism and democracy have an especially tense, often tenuous, coexistence in poor democracies. One result is a remarkable opportunity in the early twenty-first century to revisit the rough and ready days of early capitalism, whose "bloodstained story of economic individualism and unrestrained capitalist competition," in the words of Isaiah Berlin, has faded from the memory of the West.

That story involves, among other things, the brutality with which the rich democracies rid themselves of surplus classes, most conspicuously the subsistence farmer and the independent artisan made obsolete by the Industrial Revolution. The pioneer of large-scale industrial capitalism, merry England, where eight out of ten subsistence farmers were forced off the land in the thirty years between about 1780 and 1810, traveled the road to industrialization over the bodies of farmers and urban poor—pauperized, arrested as vagabonds, branded, hanged, or shipped to the colonies. The author of the classic account of the various paths to modern democracy, Barrington Moore, wrote that "as part of the industrial revolution, [England] eliminated the peasant question from English politics. The admitted brutality of the enclosures confronts us with the limitations on the possibility of peaceful transition to democracy and reminds us of open and violent conflicts that have preceded its establishment."

In their leap to modernity and global capitalism, the poor democracies have had to start out with backward, autarkic, often militarized state-owned economies. Their surplus labor is concentrated in the civil service and obsolete industries: shipyards, steel mills, mines, or defense. In the 1980s, an estimated 30 percent of the Soviet economy was assumed to be value-subtracting or, to use the fashionable term, "virtual," meaning that the finished product was worth less than the raw materials and labor that went into making it. The 2000 survey by the McKinsey Global Institute (the best study of the Russian economy to date) confirmed that estimate, finding 30 percent of Russian enterprises, employing 50 percent of the industrial work force, to be "not worth upgrading because they were either sub-scale or relied on obsolete technology."

Admittedly, Russia, with its extraordinary isolation and the militarization of its economy, is an extreme example; but every poor democracy that has implemented market reforms has experienced an initial large drop in GDP. The result has been surplus workers in obsolete bureaucracies and industries—be they Brazilian civil servants, Romanian miners, or the dockworkers of Gdańsk—creating an enormous political problem. For unlike the predemocratic capitalist West, the poor democracies have not brutally "eliminated" these millions of people from politics, but instead have given them the right to shape the institutions and practices of emerging capitalism. They vote.

The dynamics of capitalism-by-majority are by now well known. Parliaments, often dominated by leftist populists, adopt budgets with ever greater "social spending" and subsidies for loss-making public or nominally private enterprises with politically sensitive constituencies, such as farmers or coal miners. In the absence of tax revenues even remotely commensurate with skyrocketing expenditures, budget deficits burgeon (Poland, leader of the postcommunist transition, runs a budget deficit of 8 percent of GDP), national currencies weaken, interest rates rise, and governments become heavily indebted to the international financial institutions.

> *"Democracy has endowed these countries with remarkable strength and flexibility."*

In the worst-case scenario, the vicious circle closes, as governments seek to make ends meet by cutting their budgets, selling debt at astronomically high rates of return, and increasing already unrealistically high taxes. There follow depressed equity prices, stifled direct investment in the economy, capital flight, the shift of ever more economic activity into "gray" or "black" markets—and the further shrinking of the tax base. The government is confronted with a Hobson's choice, reigniting inflation by printing money or reducing already meager welfare benefits and cutting government services, with the attendant risk of losing elections to the Left (in the post-Soviet regimes, the ex-, reformed, or neo-Communists).

> *"With just a few exceptions . . . poor democracies have resisted slipping back into authoritarianism."*

The principal agent seeking to reconcile democracy and capitalism in poor democracies is the state. This is an enormous task. Almost always impoverished (and often near-bankrupt), the state is saddled with the task of simultaneously promoting modern capitalism open to the global economy and coping with the huge political problems such a strategy engenders in a democracy. Thus, in 1999, Brazil sought to reduce the budget deficit (much of it due to the salaries, benefits, and pensions of a bloated civil service) by taxing pensions and imposing painful across-the-board public sector cuts. To overcome the same problem, in the spring of 2000, Argentina cut the wages of public sector workers by 10 percent to 15 percent.

Much to the annoyance of Western journalists and experts, the capitalism-by-majority practiced by poor democracies has turned out to be a very tricky business, characterized by slow and zigzagging market reforms, incomplete privatization, a less than wholehearted embrace of globalism, and at best extreme difficulty in reducing huge budget deficits resulting from social spending and the subsidization of failed industries.

Competitive and Honest Elections

Given these heavy handicaps, it would be easy to conclude that the poor democracies, however numerous, are a flash in the pan, destined to go down in history as a hopeful but short-lived post–cold war phenomenon, too exotic to be stable, lacking the "software" of democracy, corroded by corruption, and torn apart by the tensions between democracy and capitalism.

Yet the evidence is otherwise. Democracy has endowed these countries with remarkable strength and flexibility. This was made plain in the 1997–1998 "emerging markets" financial crisis. Poor democracies like Russia, Brazil, and South Korea survived rather easily, while the nondemocracy Indonesia saw state authority collapse amid riots and anti-Chinese pogroms, and the pseudodemocracy Malaysia reached for scapegoats and kangaroo trials to save the regime.

Even where poor democracies have been systematically subverted, their democratic elements have proved difficult to extinguish. Cases in point are countries whose political systems combine antidemocratic and democratic practices and institutions, with neither side scoring a permanent victory: for instance, Belarus,

Zimbabwe, Haiti, and Pakistan. They also include "soft" one-party states or military dictatorships, like Mexico until Vicente Fox's victory in 2000 or Turkey today, where the opposition is permitted to exist but never to win the majority in the national parliament or to hold the highest executive office for long.

In 2000, three such nations passed the ultimate test: a democratic transfer of power. In Mexico, Ghana, and Yugoslavia, the opposition was able to dislodge a government by majority vote, ending, respectively, the seventy-one-year, nineteen-year, and thirteen-year rule of one party or an elected autocrat.

The case of Zimbabwe is, if anything, still more impressive and heartening. A deafening agitprop campaign and open harassment of the opposition by the government failed in the face of determined and at times heroic voter resistance. First, in a referendum in February 2000, Zimbabweans defeated a draft constitution that would have legitimized president Robert Mugabe's life term in office and authorized the seizure of land belonging to white farmers. Then in parliamentary elections in June 2000 came the spectacular success of the Movement for Democratic Change, and four months later, an attempt to impeach Mugabe, who had ruled the country since its independence in 1980.

Belarus may be another instance of deadlock between democracy and authoritarianism. Although its most recent parliamentary elections were boycotted by the opposition, there is a distinct possibility that in the next presidential election the opposition to president Alexander Lukashenko will unite behind a single candidate. "Sen'ya—Miloshavich, zaytra—Luka" (today—Milosevic, tomorrow—Lukashenko), read a poster carried by a Minsk protester in October 2000.

Countries like Yugoslavia, Ghana, and Zimbabwe have tested and confirmed the correctness of Joseph Schumpeter's classic minimalist definition of democracy: "free competition for a free vote." In his Capitalist Revolution, Peter Berger elaborated: In democracies, "governments are constituted by majority votes in regular and uncoerced elections, in which there is 'genuine competition' for votes of the electorate; and those who are engaged in such competition are guaranteed freedom of speech and freedom of association." The end result is the "institutionalized limitation of the power of government."

Freedom to vote for opposition candidates has turned out to be not only a necessary but often the sufficient condition for an initial democratic breakthrough. More or less fair elections, a press free of government censorship, real choices before the voters, and mostly honest tallying of

> *"The progress of the poor democracies in the coming years is our best hope for diminishing poverty and violence in the world."*

the results may be key to the exercise of popular sovereignty, even in the absence of (or with glaring deficiencies in) such components of mature liberal democracy as independent and impartial courts, the separation of powers, and checks and balances.

Among the most spectacular confirmations of this theory are Solidarity's parliamentary victory in Poland in 1989 and the upset of the Sandinista government by the United National Opposition in Nicaragua in 1990. Even when competitive elections and an honest count are confined to a few pockets within a dictatorial regime, they can portend earth-shattering change—as in the mighty strides made by pro-independence and anti-Communist candidates in elections in the Soviet republics between 1988 and 1991, or the election of Boris Yeltsin to the Congress of People's Deputies in March 1989 with 92 percent of the Moscow vote after Yeltsin had been expelled from the Politburo by Gorbachev. Variations on this scenario were played out in February 2000 legislative elections in Iran, when reformers and moderates won a number of districts and carried Tehran decisively, and again in the June 2001 presidential election, when the allegedly proreform president Mohammad Khatami was reelected with 76 percent of the national vote. Similarly, in March 2001 municipal elections in Ivory Coast, opposition candidates for mayor won in most cities after an almost forty-year monopoly by the ruling party. (On the other hand, in 2001 elections in Uganda and Benin, the lack of a clean vote count precluded what might have been two more democratic breakthroughs.)

Assisting Poor Democracies

What are the policy implications? First, the strength of the democratic impulse alive in poor democracies should never be underestimated. Again and again, liberty's appeal has proved powerful enough to overcome great obstacles. Elites, professing to know how the masses really feel, have time and again predicted disillusionment with democracy and its abandonment by the citizens of poor nations. Yet, in the past decade, with just a few exceptions (several African nations where democracy has been brutally and cynically subverted by warlords fanning tribal strife, and possibly Venezuela), poor democracies have resisted slipping back into authoritarianism.

Second, after almost a century of modern democracy, many Western experts and journalists have forgotten that democracy is not an all-or-nothing affair, but a system toward which a political culture may advance in fits and starts, amid contradictory impulses, by minute but cumulatively momentous steps. Experience has shown again and again that progress can defy enormous odds. This reality suggests how misleading is the term "illiberal democracy," popularized by Fareed Zakaria; a more accurate classification would be "preliberal democracy."

Third, we can revise the criteria by which the progress of poor democracies is measured. So pervasive has the Marxist interpretation of history become that economic growth is often considered the sole measure of progress. With rare exceptions, Western media coverage of poor democracies is shaped by GDP fetishism.

As always in matters of liberty, ordinary people have proved far wiser, and infinitely more patient, than intellectuals. The poor democracies have shown remarkable resilience under the harsh conditions of primitive capitalism. The voters in the poor democracies seem to have grasped—as have few journalists or experts—the essence of Isaiah Berlin's adage, "Liberty is liberty, not equality, or justice, or culture, or human happiness or a quiet conscience." Democracy itself, conceptually uncoupled from economic hardship, is cherished by consistent and solid majorities.

Corruption is a huge problem, and political cultures formed over centuries and misshapen in recent decades by particularly dehumanizing and irrational political and economic systems cannot be remade overnight. But the proper response to the inadequacies of poor democracies is neither to give up on their democratic prospects nor to refrain from pointing out their shortcomings. Rather, it is to encourage their democratic development while refusing to reduce their complex reality to a single issue or measure their progress by a single criterion. In addition, analysts must learn to recognize gradations of corruption—to differentiate between levels potentially fatal to democracy and liberal capitalism (the Nigerian or, until a few years ago, Sicilian level) and pernicious but nonlethal degrees (the Indian, Mexican, or Turkish level).

Finally, in assessing the viability and prospects of this or that poor democracy, we tend to focus on the state, which is readily analyzable, rather than on other more elusive yet crucial parts of the picture: civil society and those aspects of economic and social development that lie beyond the state's reach. The case of one rich democracy, Italy, suggests the limitations of this approach. A leading member of Silvio Berlusconi's parliamentary coalition (triumphant in the May 13, 2001, elections) recently described the contrast between "public" Italy—which he called "bad" and "embarrassing," its legal system a "joke," its armed forces "just collecting their pay," its police "pitiful"—and "private" Italy, which he called "very good," "admired all over the world," and which in the past half-century has boasted the most vibrant, least recession-prone economy in Europe. It may be that some poor democracies will follow the "Italian path" to modernity, enduring a dysfunctional state—corrupt, wasteful, meddlesome, universally despised, and cheated by the taxpayers—while enjoying a vigorous private economy.

The progress of the poor democracies in the coming years is our best hope for diminishing poverty and violence in the world. If the West is serious about assisting them, Western leaders, public opinion, and international financial institutions must be prepared to travel a long and tortuous road. It may help to remember that, unlike the West at a comparable stage of economic development, these poor countries are practicing an early capitalism that is strengthened and made more equitable by democracy, step by painful step. Surely the poor democracies—inspired, after all, by the example of the older and wealthier democracies—deserve aid and encouragement, not neglect and disdain.

Democracy Can Succeed in the Arab World

by Hussein A. Hassouna

About the author: *Hussein A. Hassouna is the ambassador of the League of Arab States to the United Nations and to the United States.*

In our day and age, democracy is the only acceptable form of government. Arab and African participants at the Africa-Europe summit held under the aegis of the Organization of African Unity and the European Union in April 2000, recognized under the Cairo Declaration the necessity of democratization, while condemning all anti-democratic forms of succession to power. Despite this commitment, Westerners continuously question the prospect of democratization in the Arab world and Africa. The Arab world is perceived as basically "undemocratic," unable to adapt to the global challenges of the democratic process. Though this view is even shared by Arab intellectuals, it overlooks the root causes of the present situation and the significant evolution that is taking place. The purpose of this essay is to shed some light on this difficult challenge.

First, we should reach an understanding on basic definitions. Are we concerned with political, economic, or social democracy? Do we assume a Western style of democracy? Is democracy equivalent to good governance? Is there an ideal democratic form? Does democracy presuppose transparency, accountability, and participation, or is it only contingent on holding elections and universal suffrage? These questions do not always have clear answers. Democracy is considered by the United Nations to imply acceptance of intellectual and political pluralism within groups, and the chance for individuals to develop their own identity, culture, and language.

On the other hand, good governance is increasingly associated with democracy, the ideal model of good governance being a competent, decentralized government that is accountable for its acts. But is this all that is needed to achieve democracy? If good governance is the right way to govern and develop economic and social policies, who then is entitled to determine which is the "right way," the West or each country according to its own culture and experiences?

The West, to be sure, encourages others to follow its example. But if we look at the ongoing soul-searching in Western societies, we may wonder what the right democratic path is. In France, we witness allegations of presidential corruption. In the United States, many question the validity of the electoral system and the partisanship of the judiciary. In Israel, which is inspired by Western models, peace advocates are alarmed by the continuous occupation of Arab lands and the discrimination to which Israeli Arabs are subjected.

The situation in the Arab world raises still more puzzling doubts among Arab intellectuals. Where are there genuine democratic institutions with real power? Does there exist a credible opposition in the majority of the Arab states? When will the emergency laws and regulations enforced in some Arab states be abrogated, or are military courts still necessary even in peacetime? Should amnesty be granted to all political prisoners, thus allowing them to reintegrate in society? Does there exist an unlimited and unchecked right to criticize a government, stage a strike, or be politically active? This questioning by the Arab intelligentsia reflects paradoxical and conflicting urges for democratization on one hand, and for internal stability on the other.

Indeed, internal stability has become the paramount priority for Arab governments, notwithstanding a remarkable overall improvement in this area. The threat of military coups has abated. Military regimes have evolved into civilian governments. In a number of countries, succession has lately occurred smoothly without major convulsion. For the most part, the Arab world has been immune from the turmoil that has affected different parts of Africa.

Potential Obstacles to Arab Democracy

Even so, some political scientists, notably Samuel P. Huntington, suggest that Islam is not hospitable to democracy. But there is no real contradiction between Islam and democracy; in fact Muslims consider Islam to be the oldest form of democracy. The Koran asserts the concept of Shura, or consultation, signifying that the leader must consult his followers and rule with their consent. This is a basic tenet of Islam and a major element of democracy. Muslim leaders have not always respected this tenet, but that does not derogate the principle itself. In reality, there is no contradiction between the Islamic system of government and the Western system.

> *"There is no real contradiction between Islam and democracy."*

Finally, when examining the question of democracy, we must bear in mind that there is no uniformity among Arab states. Egypt has 7,000 years of recorded history. Iraq, Syria, and Yemen were centers of great civilizations in the past. But most other Arab countries are relatively new, having become sovereign states only after the Second World War. When the League of Arab States was created in 1945, there were 7 independent member states; there are now 22. Some Arab countries are monarchies, while others are republics with established parliaments. Some were colonized by the French, others by the British or the Italians. And although Arabs are tied by common affinities of culture and heritage, there are also many differences among them, which reflect their level of democratization.

In truth, the Arab world needs to overcome many challenges before it can successfully democratize. The colonial legacy, the Arab-Israeli conflict, socio-economic factors, and fundamentalism are all major obstacles to democratization. Most democratic societies have evolved over time, often having faced formidable hurdles

"The global wave of democratization is helping the process of opening up Arab politics."

along the way. The United States, for instance, had to resolve the contradiction of allowing slavery while claiming to be a democracy. It then had to confront the Jim Crow laws that deprived African Americans of their right to vote. Even today there is controversy over the electoral system.

During the colonial era, the European imperial powers failed to create viable democratic institutions in their Arab possessions. To maintain their grip on this strategically important region, they relied on the leaders, while neglecting the majority of the people. As a result, many newly independent Arab states had to develop their own political culture before laying the foundation for successful democratic institutions. In some cases, colonial powers also neglected to delimit the borders between the countries they ruled, thus implanting the root cause of border conflicts in the Gulf region and North Africa.

The Arab-Israeli problem, one of the longest and bitterly emotional conflicts of the twentieth century—and now of the new century—not only influenced the process of democratization but has had a serious impact on the development of the entire region. Successive Arab-Israeli wars resulted in the rise of military regimes. National security became a primary concern, often at the expense of democratization. While democratization alone will not put an end to that conflict, a just and lasting solution will obviously have a significant impact on the successful democratization of the Arab world.

Socio-economic factors also come into play. The majority of Arab states are developing countries in which illiteracy rates remain very high, so that a large segment of the population can not truly participate in any meaningful political debate. Illiteracy, poverty, and unemployment have lead to despair and frustration. Education is therefore a top priority, and the reform of educational systems is seriously underway in most Arab countries. Food and water shortages are also major problems. In their struggle to deal with these pressing economic concerns, Arab countries often neglect the development of democratic institutions.

Fundamentalism is another internal factor that has created constraints on the progress of democracy. Governments sought to protect themselves and the people from radical Islamic fundamentalists, who often resort to terrorism to achieve their ends. Egypt, for instance, witnessed a wave of violence and political assassinations in the 1990s. The government confronted that challenge with a carrot-and-stick policy. While it cracked down on extremists, it allowed some fundamentalists to join in mainstream politics. The latter won a number of seats in the last parliamentary elections. Islamic groups were also allowed to express their criticism of government policy in newspapers, providing additional incentives for those groups to become involved in the political process rather than threaten internal stability.

On the Path to Democracy

The Arab world is rapidly moving on the path to democracy despite the weight of these challenges. Most Arab states have included structural adjustments and economic liberalization to their agendas. There is increasing respect for human rights, for freedom of speech, and for an active civil society. The global wave of democratization is helping the process of opening up Arab politics.

The League of Arab States created the Committee on Human Rights in 1968, and it adopted a human rights charter in 1994. Egypt is developing a national council on human rights, and one such already exists in Morocco. Overall, the culture of human rights may not yet be as advanced as in other democratic countries, but Arabs value the progress that is being made and are using every opportunity to see that it is encouraged according to their cultural and religious heritage.

In Syria, Morocco, Bahrain, Qatar, and Jordan, we now have young rulers who have announced their respect for human rights and have demonstrated it in concrete terms. Jordan has already declared it will create a national action plan following international standards. We cannot expect their systems to change instantly and dramatically, but it is clear that the new leaders intend to respect human rights.

The related matter of women's rights in the Middle East is a controversial subject. The status of women varies enormously from society to society, but as a general rule, the status of women and their access to education and healthcare is improving. The status of women in the Gulf states is slowly changing for the better, especially in Qatar, Bahrain, and Oman. In Egypt, women have struggled for their rights since the beginning of the twentieth century under the guidance of such well-known feminists as Dorreya Chafiq and Huda Sharawi. And today, Egyptian women from all walks of life play an active role in Egyptian society. Tunisian women enjoy rights not yet obtained in other North African countries.

Freedom of speech is essential to the development of democracy. Arab public opinion can no longer be controlled by leaders. Nor can Arab governments ignore public opinion on matters concerning the Arab world, such as supporting the Palestinian people or expressing sympathy for the people of Iraq.

The Arab press is also proving more credible and effective, and governments are becoming less restrictive with respect to the media. Jon Alterman, of the United States Institute of Peace, has found that the Arab press has become far more accurate, objective, and open to new ideas than it was before the Gulf War. He cites the increasing competition between the local, regional, and global media. For example, the Gazira channel, an Arab news network from Qatar, features secularists debating Islamists, Kuwaitis debating Iraqis, and even Palestinians and Israelis.

Following the global trend, there are an increasing number of nongovernmental organizations (NGOs) that are beginning to have an effect on Arab civil society. Modern associations have existed in the Arab world since the late nineteenth century, although civil society as a rule is still fragile. Most early associations focused on providing education and healthcare to the needy. While many local NGOs retain this traditional focus, there are increasing numbers of associations concerned with nontraditional issues.

In Egypt, the Association for the Protection of the Environment in Heliopolis was organized as a result of a local council's inadequacies. The intifada [Arab-Israeli conflict] has stimulated Palestinian associations devoted to human rights. Across the Arab world one finds women's rights groups, organizations defending the rights of minorities, and associations whose purpose it is to raise people's civic consciousness. It must be said that most of these organizations are relatively new, fragile, and sometimes subject to government supervision. Even so, the major elements of democracy are being addressed by the Arab world, and progress continues despite the turbulence that haunts the region.

The United States Should Promote Democracy in Developing Nations

by the United States Agency for International Development

About the author: *The United States Agency for International Development (USAID) is an independent agency of the federal government that extends assistance to countries recovering from disaster, trying to escape poverty, and engaging in democratic reforms.*

With the fall of the Berlin Wall, the demise of the Soviet Union, and the passing of communism as a threat to nations around the world, U.S. foreign policy moved into a new era. No longer does the United States have one clearly defined adversary, and thus no one measure by which to calibrate foreign policy worldwide. While they may be more diffuse, dangers and threats to peace, stability, and economic prosperity persist in this new era. As President George W. Bush noted in his inaugural address: "Our democratic faith is more than the creed of our country, it is the inborn hope of our humanity, an ideal we carry but do not own, a trust we bear and pass along. And even after nearly 225 years, we have a long way yet to travel." The challenge now is to recognize and understand multiple and constantly-shifting sources of peril and to address complex and inter-linked causes of unrest such as ethnic strife, environmental degradation, rapid population growth, and poor economic performance, so that we may take advantage of new opportunities.

"The Motive Force for Freedom and Democracy"

One of these opportunities is to promote principles of democratic governance and provide technical assistance to newly formed democracies. USAID works to encourage democracy in developing nations throughout the world partly on the intrinsic value which rests in the ideals of liberty, personal and civic freedom, and government of, for, and by the people: ideals on which the United

Excerpted from "Democracy & the U.S. National Interest," by the United States Agency for International Development, www.usaid.gov, 2002.

States was founded and which continue to gird the social and political life of our nation. Secretary of State Colin Powell noted in his confirmation hearing that a foremost principle of the Bush Administration's foreign policy will be

> . . . that America stands ready to help any country that wishes to join the democratic world—any country that puts the rule of law in place and begins to live by the rule, any country that seeks peace and prosperity and a place in the sun. In that light, there is no country on earth that is not touched by America, for we have become the motive force for freedom and democracy in the world.

By promoting and assisting the growth of democracy, the United States also supports the emergence and establishment of polities that will become better trade partners and more stable governments. In his speech before the 2001 Annual Meeting of the Bretton Woods committee, Secretary of State Powell commented on this relationship, noting that business and goverments alike ". . . must realize that openness, transparency and good government are the building blocks of a healthy investment climate. Political and economic reform must go hand in hand if either is to succeed."

"America stands ready to help any country that wishes to join the democratic world."

Smooth transitions of power will reduce the deadly risk of nuclear weapons falling to the control of irrational agents. By facilitating citizens' trust in their government, democracy may also prevent hundreds of thousands of individuals from fleeing their homelands and contributing to destabilizing and costly refugee flows, anarchy and failed states, and the spread of disease and epidemics of catastrophic proportion.

America's strategic long-term domestic and foreign policy objectives are best served by enlarging the community of democratic nations worldwide. Establishing democratic institutions, free and open markets, an informed and educated populace, a vibrant civil society, and a relationship between state and society that encourages pluralism, participation, and peaceful conflict resolution—all of these contribute to the goal of establishing sustainable democracies.

The Agency's Strategic Plan, adopted in 1997, identifies four strategic objectives in the democracy sector:

• Rule of Law
• Elections & Political Processes
• Civil Society
• Governance

Progress toward all four objectives is necessary to achieve sustainable democracy.

The Rule of Law and the Importance of Elections

Rule of Law. The term "rule of law" embodies the basic principles of equal treatment of all people before the law, fairness, and both constitutional and actual guarantees of basic human rights. A predictable legal system with fair, transparent, and effective judicial institutions is essential to the protection of citizens against the arbitrary use of state authority and lawless acts of both organizations and individuals. In many states with weak or nascent democratic traditions, existing laws are not equitable or equitably applied; judicial independence is compromised; individual and minority rights are not truly guaranteed; and institutions have not yet developed the capacity to administer existing laws. Weak legal institutions endanger democratic reform and sustainable development in developing countries.

Without the rule of law, a state lacks (a) the legal framework necessary for civil society to flourish; (b) adequate checks on the executive and legislative branches of government; and (c) necessary legal foundations for free and fair electoral and political processes. Beyond the democracy and governance sector, the accomplishment of other USAID goals relies on effective rule of law. For example, civil and commercial codes that respect private property and contracts are key ingredients for the development of market-based economies. USAID's efforts to strengthen legal systems fall under three inter-connected priority areas: supporting legal reform, improving the administration of justice, and increasing citizens' access to justice.

Elections and Political Processes. Free and fair elections are integral to a functioning democracy. Regional and country-specific situations sometimes require the staging of national elections within limited time-frames.

Examples include countries emerging out of protracted civil war or countries whose governments have lost the confidence of their citizens. Such situations require focused efforts and rapid response logistical, administrative, and training capabilities. USAID provides rapid response capabilities in the following areas: conducting pre-election assessments; training election commissions; training poll watchers and/or providing assistance to other polling officials; identifying, developing, and procuring election commodities; training indigenous and/or international election observers; developing civic and voter education techniques; training election officials, legislators, and government leaders; and developing programs to address gender, minority, and ethnic issues. The focus on this intervention is short-term, i.e., the successful conduct of a given election.

More generally, the problems that exist in newly emerging democracies include a weak institutional capacity to support, organize, and carry out elections; poorly organized political parties; and a lack of knowledge and understanding by citizens of the political process, electoral process, and the mechanics of voting. USAID programs to address these problems include election planning and implementation, political party development, voter education, and support for domestic and international monitoring groups. These efforts focus increasingly on the long-term institutionalization of appropriate political procedures through the strengthening of local capacity.

Chapter 4

Civil Society and Governance

Civil Society. The hallmark of a free society is the ability of individuals to associate with like-minded individuals, express their views publicly, openly debate public policy, and petition their government. "Civil society" is an increasingly accepted term which best describes the non-governmental, not-for-profit, independent nature of this segment of society. In countries with fragile democratic traditions, the freedoms so necessary to building and sustaining an active and independent civil society often are little understood, temporarily curtailed, or simply denied. USAID is working to strengthen commitment to an independent and politically active civil society in developing countries. The range of groups receiving USAID assistance includes coalitions of professional associations, civic education groups, women's rights organizations, business and labor federations, media groups, bar associations, environmental activist groups, and human rights monitoring organizations.

Also of great significance is the Agency's support for democratic and independent trade unions. In most countries, trade unions are the largest and most inclusive grassroots organizations. Consequently, they are instrumental in fostering the development and consolidation of democracy. In many countries, free and independent trade unions have been vocal opponents of repression and, in many cases, at the forefront of the democracy movement.

Governance. A key determinant for successful democratic consolidation is the ability of democratically-elected governments to provide "good governance." While many citizens of developing countries value characteristics associated with democracy (e.g., elections, human rights, and representation), they are often equally interested in qualities such as public accountability, responsiveness, transparency, and efficiency. "Good governance" assumes a government's ability to maintain social peace, guarantee law and order, promote or create conditions necessary for economic growth, and ensure a minimum level of social security. Yet many new governments fail to realize the long-term benefits of adopting effective governance policies. Even in cases where governments recognize the value of such policies, they often lack the capacity to implement them. For these reasons, newly democratic governments too often revert to more familiar patterns of authoritarianism and abuse.

Because the behavior of formal state actors can support or undermine developmental and democratic processes, USAID works to encourage and assist young democratic governments to reform their structures and processes to make them more transparent, accountable, and participatory. USAID works to encourage more transparent and accountable government institutions in five areas: governmental integrity; democratic decentralization; legislative strengthening; civil-military relations; and effective policy implementation.

Some Developing Nations Do Not Have Cultures That Support Democracy

by Lawrence E. Harrison

About the author: *Lawrence E. Harrison directed USAID missions in five Latin American countries between 1965 and 1981. He is a senior fellow at Harvard University's Academy for International and Area Studies and co-editor of* Culture Matters: How Values Shape Human Progress.

The decades-old war on poverty and authoritarianism in the poor countries of Africa, Asia and Latin America has produced more disappointment and frustration than it has victories. The deprivation and despair that prevailed in the mid-twentieth century persist in most of these countries, even a decade after capitalism's ideological triumph over socialism. Where democratically elected chiefs of state have displaced traditional authoritarian regimes, a pattern most notable in Latin America, the experiments are fragile, and "democracy" often means little more than periodic elections.

What explains the persistence of poverty and authoritarianism? Why have they proven so intractable? Why have no countries in Africa, Asia and Latin America other than the East Asian dragons [Asian nations that have performed well economically] made their way into the elite group of affluent countries? The conventional diagnoses that have been offered during the past half century—exploitation, imperialism, education and know-how shortfalls, lack of opportunity, lack of capital, inadequate markets, weak institutions—are demonstrably inadequate. The crucial element that has been largely ignored is the cultural: that is to say, values and attitudes that stand in the way of progress. Some cultures, above all those of the West and East Asia, have proven themselves more prone to progress than others. Their achievements are reiterated when their peoples migrate to other countries, as in the cases of the British in the United States, Canada, Australia and New Zealand; and the Chinese,

Japanese and Koreans, who have flourished wherever they have migrated.

The conclusion that culture matters goes down hard. It clashes with cultural relativism, widely subscribed to in the academic world, which argues that cultures can be assessed only on their own terms and that value judgments by outsiders are taboo. The implication is that all cultures are equally worthy, and those who argue to the contrary are often labeled ethnocentric, intolerant or even racist. A similar problem is encountered with those economists who believe that culture is irrelevant—that people will respond to economic signals in the same way regardless of their culture.

But a growing number of academics, journalists and politicians are writing and talking about culture as a crucial factor in societal development, and a new paradigm of human progress is emerging. Federal Reserve Chairman Alan Greenspan captured the shift recently when he said, in the context of economic conditions in Russia, that he had theretofore assumed that capitalism was "human nature." But in the wake of the collapse of the Russian economy, he concluded that "it was not human nature at all, but culture"—a succinct restatement of [sociologist] Max Weber's thesis in *The Protestant Ethic and the Spirit of Capitalism*.

A Dismal Record

In the 1950s, the world turned its attention from rebuilding the countries devastated by World War II to ending the poverty, ignorance and injustice in which most of the peoples of Africa, Asia and Latin America lived. Optimism abounded in the wake of the stunning success of the Marshall Plan [a plan named after U.S. general George Marshall to aid Europe after World War II] in Western Europe and Japan's ascent from the ashes of defeat. Development was viewed as inevitable, particularly as the colonial yoke disappeared. Walt Rostow's hugely influential book, *The Stages of Economic Growth*, published in 1960, suggested that human progress was driven by a dialectic that could be accelerated. The Alliance for Progress, John F. Kennedy's answer to the Cuban revolution, captured the prevailing optimism. It would duplicate the Marshall Plan's success, and Latin America would be well on its way to prosperity and democracy within ten years.

But as the century ended, that optimism had been displaced by frustration and pessimism, the consensus on market economics and democracy notwithstanding. Spain, Portugal, South Korea, Taiwan, Singapore and the former British colony Hong Kong have followed Rostow's trajectory into the First World, and a few others—for example, Chile, China, Malaysia and Thailand—have experienced sustained, rapid growth. Spain and Portugal finally opened themselves to the Enlightenment, the Industrial Revolution and the Western values that had driven the modernization of their neighbors in Eu-

> *"Some cultures, above all those of the West and East Asia, have proven themselves more prone to progress than others."*

rope. And like Japan before them, the East Asian dragons rode the Protestant Ethic-like features of Confucianism and export promotion policies to success.

But the vast majority of countries still lags far behind. Of the six billion people who inhabit the world today, fewer than one billion are to be found in the advanced democracies. More than four billion live in what the World Bank classifies as "low-income" or "lower middle-income" countries. The quality of life in those countries is dismaying:

• Half or more of the adult population of 23 countries, mostly in Africa, is illiterate. Non-African countries include Afghanistan, Bangladesh, Nepal, Pakistan and Haiti.

• Half or more of the women in 35 countries are illiterate, including not only those countries just listed but Algeria, Egypt, Guatemala, India, Laos, Morocco, Nigeria and Saudi Arabia.

• Life expectancy is below 60 years in 45 countries, most in Africa, but also Afghanistan, Cambodia, Haiti, Laos and Papua New Guinea. Life expectancy is below 50 years in 18 countries, all in Africa. And in Sierra Leone it is just 37 years.

• The mortality rate for children under 5 is greater than 10 percent in at least 35 countries, most, again, in Africa. Other countries include Bangladesh, Bolivia, Haiti, Laos, Nepal, Pakistan and Yemen.

• The population growth rate in the poorest countries is 2.1 percent annually, three times the rate in the high-income countries. The growth rate in some Islamic countries is astonishingly high: 5 percent in Oman, 4.9 percent in the United Arab Emirates, 4.8 percent in Jordan, 3.4 percent in Saudi Arabia and Turkmenistan.

Furthermore, the most inequitable income distribution patterns among countries supplying such data to the World Bank—not all do—are found in the poorer countries, particularly in Latin America and Africa. The most affluent 10 percent of Brazil's population accounts for almost 48 percent of its income. Kenya, South Africa and Zimbabwe are a fraction of a point behind.

Democratic institutions are commonly weak or nonexistent in Africa, the Islamic countries of the Middle East, and in the rest of Asia. Democracy has appeared to prosper in Latin America over the past fifteen years. Argentina, Brazil and Chile seem headed toward democratic stability after decades of military rule. But the fragility of the democratic experiments is underscored by recent events in several countries: in Colombia, where left-wing guerrillas, often cooperating with drug traffickers, control large parts of the country and threaten to topple the government; in Ecuador, where ineptitude and corruption in the Andean capital of Quito have contributed to a deep recession and to separatist sentiment in coastal Guayaquil; and in Venezuela, where Hugo Chávez, an officer who attempted two coups in the early 1990s, is now president and conducting himself in ways that leave one wondering whether he, and not Fidel Castro, may turn out to be the last Latin American caudillo. And there remains a weighty question: Why after more than 150 years of independence has Latin America, an extension of the West, failed to consolidate democratic institutions?

In sum, the world at the beginning of the twenty-first century is far poorer, far more unjust, far more authoritarian than most people half a century ago expected it would be, and the anticipated fruits of the post–Cold War democratic-capitalist consensus have, with a few exceptions, yet to be harvested.

Explaining the Failure: Colonialism and Dependency

As it became apparent that the problems of underdevelopment were more intractable than the development experts had predicted, two explanations with Marxist-Leninist roots came to dominate the politics of the poor countries and the universities of the rich countries: colonialism and dependency.

Vladimir Lenin had identified imperialism as a late and inevitable stage of capitalism that reflected what he viewed as the inability of increasingly monopolistic capitalist countries to find domestic markets for their products and capital. For those former colonies, possessions or mandate countries that had recently gained independence, imperialism was a reality that left a profound imprint on the national psyche and presented a ready explanation for underdevelopment—particularly in Africa, where national boundaries had often been arbitrarily drawn without reference to homogeneity of culture or tribal coherence.

> *"The world at the beginning of the twenty-first century is far poorer, far more unjust, far more authoritarian than most people half a century ago expected it would be."*

For those countries in what would come to be called the Third World that had been independent for a century or more, as in Latin America, "imperialism" took the shape of "dependency"—the theory that the poor countries of "the periphery" were bilked by the rich capitalist countries of "the center." These countries allegedly depressed world market prices of basic commodities and inflated the prices of manufactured goods, enabling their multinational corporations to extort excessive profits.

The injustice of dependency was popularized by the Uruguayan writer Eduardo Galeano, whose phenomenally successful book, *The Open Veins of Latin America*, was first published in 1971 (it has since been republished sixty-seven times). The following lines capture its essence: Latin America is the region of open veins. From the discovery up to the present, our wealth has been taken from us first by European capital and then by American capital and has accumulated in those distant centers of power. . . . The international division of labor consists of some countries that specialize in getting rich and some in getting poor.

The Marxist-Leninist roots of dependency theory are apparent from another popular book published in the same year with the title *Dependency and Devel-*

opment in Latin America. The authors were Fernando Henrique Cardoso, today the president of Brazil, and Enzo Faletto, an Argentine. The book, in stark contrast with President Cardoso's centrist, democratic-capitalist policies since 1993, concludes:

> It is not realistic to imagine that capitalist development will solve basic problems for the majority of the population. In the end, what has to be discussed as an alternative is not the consolidation of the state and the fullfillment of 'autonomous capitalism' but how to supersede them. The important question, then, is how to construct paths toward socialism.

Neither "colonialism" nor "dependency" have much credibility today. For many, including some Africans, the statute of limitations on colonialism as an explanation for underdevelopment lapsed long ago. Moreover, four former colonies, two British (Hong Kong and Singapore) and two Japanese (South Korea and Taiwan), have vaulted into the First World. One rarely hears dependency mentioned today, not even in American universities, where not many years ago it was a conventional wisdom that brooked no dissent. Contributing to dependency theory's demise were, among other factors, the collapse of communism in Eastern Europe; the transformation of communism in China into conventional, increasingly free-market authoritarianism; the collapse of the Cuban economy after Russia halted massive Soviet subventions; the success of the East Asian dragons in the world market; the decisive defeat of the Sandinistas in the 1990 Nicaraguan elections; and theretofore stridently anti-Yanqui Mexico's initiative to join Canada and the United States in North American Free Trade Agreement (NAFTA).

And so an explanatory vacuum emerged in the last decade of the century.

Explaining the Failure: Culture

Largely unnoticed in U.S. academic circles, a new, inward-looking paradigm that focuses on cultural values and attitudes is gradually filling the explanatory vacuum left by dependency theory's collapse. Recently, Latin America has taken the lead in articulating the paradigm and contriving initiatives to translate it into actions designed not only to accelerate economic growth but also to fortify democratic institutions and promote social justice. The culture paradigm also has adherents in Africa and Asia.

Of course, many analysts who have studied the East Asian economic miracles over the past three decades have concluded that "Confucian" values—such as emphasis on the future, work, education, merit and frugality—have played a crucial role in East Asia's successes. But just as the flourishing of the East Asians in the world market—so inconsistent with dependency theory—was largely ignored by Latin American intellectuals and politicians until recent years, so was the cultural explanation for those miracles. Latin America has now for the most part accepted the economic policy lessons of East Asia, and it is confronting the question: If dependency and imperialism are not responsible for our economic underdevelopment, our authoritarian political traditions, and our extreme social injustice, what is?

That question was posed by the Venezuelan writer Carlos Rangel in a book published in the mid-1970s, *The Latin Americans: Their Love-Hate Relationship with the United States.* Rangel was not the first Latin American to conclude that traditional Ibero-American values and attitudes, and the institutions that reflected and reinforced them, were the principal cause of Latin America's "failure," a word he contrasted with the "success" of the United States and Canada. Similar conclusions were recorded by, among others, Simón Bolívar's aide, Francisco Miranda, in the last years of the eighteenth century; by the eminent Argentines Juan Bautista Alberdi and Domingo Faustino Sarmiento and the Chilean Francisco Bilbao in the second half of the nineteenth century; and by the Nicaraguan intellectual Salvador Mendieta early in the twentieth century. Anticipating similar comments by Alexis de Tocqueville twenty years later, Bolívar himself had this to say in 1815:

> *"Except for cultural factors, nothing prevented Mexico from doing what Japan did when it almost totally displaced the United States' production of television sets."*

> As long as our compatriots fail to acquire the talents and political virtues that distinguish our brothers to the north, political systems based on popular participation, far from helping us, will bring our ruin. Unfortunately, those qualities in the necessary degree are beyond us. We are dominated by the vices of Spain—violence, overweening ambition, vindictiveness, and greed.

Rangel's book earned him the enmity of most Latin American intellectuals and was mostly ignored by Latin American specialists in North America and Europe. But the book has proven to be seminal. In 1979 Nobelist Octavio Paz explained the contrast between the two Americas this way: "One, English-speaking, is the daughter of the tradition that has founded the modern world: the Reformation, with its social and political consequences, democracy and capitalism. The other, Spanish- and Portuguese-speaking, is the daughter of the universal Catholic monarchy and the Counter-Reformation."

One finds strong echoes of Rangel in Claudio Véliz's 1994 book, *The New World of the Gothic Fox*, which contrasts the Anglo-Protestant and Ibero-Catholic legacies in the New World. Véliz defines the new cultural current with the words of the celebrated Peruvian writer Mario Vargas Llosa, who asserts that the economic, educational and judicial reforms necessary to Latin America's modernization cannot be effected

> unless they are preceded or accompanied by a reform of our customs and ideas, of the whole complex system of habits, knowledge, images and forms that we understand by 'culture.' The culture within which we live and act today in Latin America is neither liberal nor is it altogether democratic. We have

democratic governments, but our institutions, our reflexes and our mentality are very far from being democratic. They remain populist and oligarchic, or absolutist, collectivist or dogmatic, flawed by social and racial prejudices, immensely intolerant with respect to political adversaries, and devoted to the worst monopoly of all, that of the truth.

The recent runaway bestseller in Latin America, *Guide to the Perfect Latin American Idiot*, is dedicated to Rangel by its co-authors, Colombian Plinio Apuleyo Mendoza; Vargas Llosa's son, Álvaro; and Cuban exile Carlos Alberto Montaner, all three of whom identify themselves as "idiots" of the far Left in their younger years. The book criticizes those Latin American intellectuals of this century who have promoted the view that the region is a victim of imperialism. Among them are Galeano, Fidel Castro, Che Guevara, pre-presidential Fernando Henrique Cardoso and Gustavo Gutiérrez, founder of Liberation Theology. Mendoza, Montaner and Vargas Llosa strongly imply that the real causes of Latin America's underdevelopment are in the minds of the Latin Americans:

> In reality, except for cultural factors, nothing prevented Mexico from doing what Japan did when it almost totally displaced the United States' production of television sets.

In their 1998 sequel, *Manufacturers of Misery*, the authors trace the influence of the traditional culture on the behavior of six elite groups: the politicians, the military, business people, the clergy, the intellectuals and the revolutionaries, all of whom have acted in ways that impede progress toward democratic-capitalist modernity. A year later, a prominent Argentine intellectual and media celebrity; Mariano Grondona, published *The Cultural Conditions of Economic Development*, which analyzes and contrasts development-prone (e.g., U.S. and Canadian) and development-resistant (e.g., Latin American) cultures. Among the differences noted was a stronger emphasis on creativity; innovation, trust, education and merit in the former.

To be sure, Latin American values and attitudes are changing, as the transition to democratic politics and market economics of the past fifteen years suggests. Several forces are modifying the region's culture, among them the new intellectual current, the globalization of communications and economics, and the surge in evangelical/Pentecostal Protestantism. Protestants now account for more than 30 percent of the population in Guatemala and 15–20 percent in Brazil, Chile and Nicaragua.

The impact of these new-paradigm books and Montaner's weekly columns (he is the most widely read columnist in the Spanish language) has been profound in Latin America. But in the United States, Canada and Western Europe, they have gone largely unnoticed. A generation of Latin Americanists nurtured on dependency theory, or the less extreme view that the solution to Latin America's problems depends on the United States being more magnanimous in its dealings with the region, finds the cultural explanation indigestible.

However, one American of Mexican descent, Texas businessman Lionel Sosa, has contributed to the new paradigm. In his 1998 book, *The Americano Dream*, Sosa catalogues a series of Hispanic values and attitudes that present obstacles to achieving the upward mobility of mainstream America:

- The resignation of the poor—"To be poor is to deserve heaven. To be rich is to deserve hell. It is good to suffer in this life because in the next life you will find eternal reward."
- The low priority given to education—"The girls don't really need it—they'll get married anyway. And the boys? It's better that they go to work, to help the family." (The Hispanic high school dropout rate in the United States is about 30 percent, vastly higher than that of white and black Americans.)
- Fatalism—"Individual initiative, achievement, self-reliance, ambition, aggressiveness—all these are useless in the face of an attitude that says, 'We must not challenge the will of God. . . . The virtues so essential to business success in the United States are looked upon as sins by the Latino church." At least in California, the Hispanic rate of self-employment is well below the state's average.
- Mistrust of those outside the family, which contributes to the generally small size of Hispanic businesses.

At least one African has come to similar conclusions about the slow rate of progress on his continent. Daniel Etounga-Manguelle is a Cameroonian who holds a doctorate in economics and planning from the Sorbonne and who heads a prominent consulting company that operates throughout Africa. In 1990 he published a book in France entitled *Does Africa Need a Cultural Adjustment Program?*, in which he attributes Africa's poverty; authoritarianism and social injustice principally to traditional cultural values and attitudes. The book evokes the new-paradigm literature in Latin America.

> *"What is needed [in Africa] is a cultural revolution that transforms traditional authoritarian child-rearing practices, which 'produce sheep.'"*

Etounga-Manguelle's analysis of African culture highlights the highly centralized, vertical traditions of authority; a focus on the past and present, not the future; a rejection of "the tyranny of time"; a distaste for work ("The African works to live but doesn't live to work"); the suppression of individual initiative, achievement and saving (the corollary is jealousy of success); a belief in sorcery that nurtures irrationality and fatalism.

For those, particularly in the international development community, who see "institution-building" as the way to solve the problems of the Third World, Etounga-Manguelle offers an insight: "Culture is the mother; institutions are the children."

Etounga-Manguelle concludes that Africa must "change or perish." A cultural "adjustment" is not enough. What is needed is a cultural revolution that transforms traditional authoritarian child-rearing practices, which "produce sheep"; transforms education through emphasis on the individual, independent judgment and creativity; produces free individuals working together for the progress of the community; produces an elite concerned with the well-being of the society; and promotes a healthy economy based on the work ethic, the profit motive and individual initiative.

How Culture Influences Progress

The idea of "progress" is suspect for those who are committed to cultural relativism. Some anthropologists view it as an idea the West is trying to impose on other cultures. At the extreme, cultural relativists may argue that Westerners have no right to criticize institutions and practices like female genital mutilation; suttee, the Hindu practice for widows to join their dead husbands on funeral pyres; or even slavery. Some Western anthropologists opposed the United Nations Universal Declaration of Human Rights.

But after a half century of the communications revolution, it is clear that progress in the Western—and East Asian—sense has become a virtually universal aspiration. I am not speaking of progress as defined by the affluent consumer society, although an end to poverty is clearly one of the universal goals, and that inevitably means higher levels of consumption. Over the almost two decades that I have been studying and writing about the relationship between cultural values and human progress, I have identified ten values, attitudes or mindsets that distinguish progressive cultures—cultures that facilitate achievement of the goals of the UN Declaration—from static cultures, which impede their achievement:

1. Time orientation: The progressive culture emphasizes the future, the static culture the present or past. Future orientation implies a progressive world-view: influence over one's destiny, rewards in this life for virtue, and positive-sum economics in which wealth expands—in contrast to the zero-sum psychology commonly found in poor countries.

2. Work and achievement are central to the good life in the progressive culture, but are of lesser importance in the static culture. In the former, work structures daily life, and diligence, creativity and achievement are rewarded not only financially but also with satisfaction, self-respect and prestige.

3. Frugality is the mother of investment—and financial security—in progressive cultures; a threat to the egalitarian status quo in static, zero-sum cultures in which one person's gains are at the expense of others.

4. Education is the key to advancement in progressive cultures but is of marginal importance except for the elites in static cultures.

5. Merit is central to advancement in the progressive culture; connections and family are what count in the static culture.

6. Community: The radius of identification and trust extends beyond the family to the broader society in the progressive culture, whereas the family circum-

scribes community in the static culture. Societies with a narrow radius of identification and trust are more prone to corruption, nepotism and tax evasion and are less likely to engage in philanthropy.

7. The societal ethical code tends to be more rigorous in the progressive culture. Every advanced democracy except Belgium, Taiwan, Italy and South Korea appears among the 25 least corrupt countries on Transparency International's "Corruption Perceptions Index." Chile and Botswana are the only Third World countries that appear among the top 25.

8. Justice and fair play are universal, impersonal expectations in the progressive culture. In the static culture, justice, like personal advancement, is often a function of whom you know or how much you can pay.

9. Authority tends toward dispersion and horizontality in progressive cultures, which encourage dissent; toward concentration and verticality in static cultures, which encourage orthodoxy.

10. Secularism: The influence of religious institutions on civic life is small in the progressive culture; their influence in static cultures is often substantial. Heterodoxy and dissent are encouraged in the former, orthodoxy and conformity are encouraged in the latter.

Obviously, these ten factors are generalized and idealized, and the reality of cultural variation is not black and white but a spectrum, in which colors fuse into one another. Few countries would be graded "10" on all the factors, just as few countries would be graded "1." Nonetheless, virtually all of the advanced democracies—and high-achieving ethnic/religious groups such as Mormons, East Asian immigrants, Jews, Sikhs and Basques—would receive substantially higher scores than virtually all of the Third World countries.

This conclusion invites the inference that what is really in play is development, not culture. The same argument could be made about Transparency International's corruption index. There is a complex interplay of cause and effect between culture and progress. But the power of culture is demonstrable— for example, in those countries where the economic achievement of ethnic minorities far exceeds that of the majorities, as in the case of the Chinese in Thailand, Indonesia, Malaysia, the Philippines and even the United States.

> *"We need to understand a good deal more about the intricate relationship between culture and progress and what can be done to promote progressive values."*

The ten factors I have suggested are not definitive. But they do at least suggest which elements in the vastness of "culture" may influence the way societies evolve. Moreover, the new-paradigm writers in Latin America and Africa attribute the slow modernization of their countries in large measure to just such traditional values and attitudes. Their views evoke the seminal culturalists Alexis de Tocqueville, Max Weber and Edward Banfield. Tocqueville's *Democ-*

racy in America is particularly relevant for those who would adduce geographic or institutional explanations for democratic development:

> Europeans exaggerate the influence of geography on the lasting powers of democratic institutions. Too much importance is attached to laws and too little to mores. . . . If in the course of this book I have not succeeded in making the reader feel the importance I attach to the practical experience of the Americans, to their habits, opinions, and, in a word, their mores, in maintaining their laws, I have failed in the main object of my work.

Changing the Traditional Culture

In part because of the influence of the new-paradigm writers, but in some cases because of life experiences that have brought them to the same conclusions, a growing number of Latin Americans and others have initiated activities that promote progressive values and attitudes.

Octavio Mavila was for three decades the Honda distributor in Peru. A burly self-made man well into his seventies, Mavila has visited Japan numerous times over the years. He came to the conclusion that the only significant difference between Japan and Peru was that Japanese children learned progressive values while Peruvian children did not. In 1990 he established the Institute of Human Development in Lima to promote "the Ten Commandments of Development": order, cleanliness, punctuality, responsibility, achievement, honesty, respect for the rights of others, respect for the law, work ethic and frugality. (In *The Americano Dream*, Lionel Sosa presents a similar program for success based on "the twelve traits of successful Latinos.") More than two million Peruvian students have participated in courses sponsored by the institute.

The Ten Commandments of Development are being preached outside Peru, too. Humberto Belli, Nicaragua's minister of education in two administrations, viewed them as central to his program of educational reform. Ramón de la Peña, rector of the Monterrey campus of Mexico's prestigious Monterrey Institute of Technology and Higher Studies, has also promoted use of the Ten Commandments.

The effectiveness of the evangelizing approach to cultural change needs to be evaluated. As Luis Ugalde, a Jesuit who is the rector of the Catholic University of Caracas, has observed, if children learn a progressive ethic in school and find it irrelevant to their lives outside of school, the impact may be scant. That is why Ugalde, who is convinced that values and attitudes matter, is promoting anti-corruption, pro-merit campaigns in government, business and the professions.

Corruption is in significant part a cultural phenomenon, linked to factors like limited radius of identification and trust that translate into a limited sense of community and an elastic ethical code. Corruption has become a high-profile issue in Latin America. In 1998 the Organization of American States adopted the Inter-American Convention against Corruption. Few expect that the Convention itself is going to dramatically reduce the incidence of corruption—five Latin American countries (Paraguay, Honduras, Colombia, Venezuela and

Ecuador) appear among Transparency International's ten most corrupt countries. But it is clear that corruption is today receiving far more attention than it once did, by, among others, the World Bank.

The gender issue has also come to the fore, challenging the traditional machismo culture. Latin American women are increasingly aware of the gender democratization that has occurred, particularly in First World countries, in recent decades, and they are increasingly organizing and taking initiatives to rectify the sexism that has traditionally kept them in second-class status. In several countries, laws concerning parental and property rights and divorce have been liberalized in favor of women, and nine countries have established obligatory quotas for women candidates in elections. While these electoral laws are not uniformly effective, they are a reminder that the gender revolution, and all that it implies with respect to transformation of traditional values, is reaching Latin America.

Integrating Values and Attitudes into Development

With the notable exceptions of East Asia and Iberia, human progress during the half century since World War II has been disheartening. The principal reason for this has been the failure to take into account the power of culture to thwart or facilitate progress. It is, for example, the cultural contrast between Western Europe and Latin America that chiefly explains the success of the Marshall Plan and the failure of the Alliance for Progress.

This is not to say that addressing culture will solve all problems. Culture is one of several factors—others being geography and climate, ideology, policies, globalization, leadership, the vagaries of history—that influence progress. The limits of cultural explanations are obvious when one considers the striking contrasts in progress between North and South Korea, and between East and West Germany. But particularly as we view the longer run, culture's power becomes more apparent.

At a 1999 Harvard symposium entitled "Cultural Values and Human Progress," Nathan Glazer observed that people are made uncomfortable or are offended by cultural explanations of why some countries and some ethnic groups do better than others. But the alternative—to view oneself or one's group as a victims—is worse. As Bernard Lewis recently observed in a *Foreign Affairs* article about the Islamic countries, When people realize that things are going wrong, there are two questions they can ask. One is, 'What did we do wrong?' and the other is 'Who did this to us?' The latter leads to conspiracy theories and paranoia. The first question leads to another line of thinking: 'How do we put it right?'

A consensus emerged at the Harvard symposium that we need to understand a good deal more about the intricate relationship between culture and progress and what can be done to promote progressive values. A research agenda has been developed, the end product of which would be guidelines for governments and development institutions. The agenda would 1) define, analyze and weigh the values that most influence development; 2) enhance understanding of the complex relationships among values, policies, institutions and development; and 3) enhance understanding of the role of agents of cultural transmission, e.g., parents, peers, schools, television. The research agenda would also extend the World Values Survey, which now covers sixty-five countries, further into the poor countries and tailor it to the results of the research on values. Finally, an evaluation would be undertaken of activities already under way that promote progressive values and attitudes, particularly through education, more effective parenting, promotion of entrepreneurship, promotion of civic responsibility, reduction of corruption and expansion of philanthropy.

Culture is not the only force that shapes the destinies of nations, particularly in the short run. Moreover, culture changes. An observation by Daniel Patrick Moynihan is apt: "The central conservative truth is that it is culture, not politics, that determines the success of a society. The central liberal truth is that politics can change a culture and save it from itself."

But I believe that David Landes is right in concluding in his recent book, *The Wealth and Poverty of Nations*, "If we learn anything from the history of economic development, it is that culture makes all the difference." I believe that the same is true of political and social development. Yet the role of cultural values and attitudes as obstacles to or facilitators of progress has been largely ignored by governments and aid agencies. Integrating value and attitude change into policies and programs will assure that, in the next fifty years, the world does not relive the poverty and injustice in which most poor countries have been mired during the past half century's "decades of development."

There Are Serious Obstacles to Freedom in the Arab World

by Bernard Lewis

About the author: *Bernard Lewis is the Cleveland E. Dodge Professor of near eastern studies at Princeton University and the author of numerous books, including* The Arabs in History, Islam and the West, *and* What Went Wrong?: Western Impact and Middle Eastern Response.

In the course of the twentieth century it became abundantly clear that things had gone badly wrong in the Middle East—and, indeed, in all the lands of Islam. Compared with Christendom, its rival for more than a millennium, the world of Islam had become poor, weak, and ignorant. The primacy and therefore the dominance of the West was clear for all to see, invading every aspect of the Muslim's public and even—more painfully—private life.

Muslim modernizers—by reform or revolution—concentrated their efforts in three main areas: military, economic, and political. The results achieved were, to say the least, disappointing. The quest for victory by updated armies brought a series of humiliating defeats. The quest for prosperity through development brought in some countries impoverished and corrupt economies in recurring need of external aid, in others an unhealthy dependence on a single resource—oil. And even this was discovered, extracted, and put to use by Western ingenuity and industry, and is doomed, sooner or later, to be exhausted, or, more probably, superseded, as the international community grows weary of a fuel that pollutes the land, the sea, and the air wherever it is used or transported, and that puts the world economy at the mercy of a clique of capricious autocrats. Worst of all are the political results: the long quest for freedom has left a string of shabby tyrannies, ranging from traditional autocracies to dictatorships that are modern only in their apparatus of repression and indoctrination.

Many remedies were tried—weapons and factories, schools and parliaments—but none achieved the desired result. Here and there they brought some alleviation and, to limited elements of the population, some benefit. But they failed to remedy or even to halt the increasing imbalance between Islam and the Western world.

There was worse to come. It was bad enough for Muslims to feel poor and weak after centuries of being rich and strong, to lose the position of leadership that they had come to regard as their right, and to be reduced to the role of followers of the West. But the twentieth century, particularly the second half, brought further humiliation—the awareness that they were no longer even the first among followers but were falling back in a lengthening line of eager and more successful Westernizers, notably in East Asia. The rise of Japan had been an encouragement but also a reproach. The later rise of other Asian economic powers brought only reproach. The proud heirs of ancient civilizations had gotten used to hiring Western firms to carry out tasks of which their own contractors and technicians were apparently incapable. Now Middle Eastern rulers and businessmen found themselves inviting contractors and technicians from Korea—only recently emerged from Japanese colonial rule—to perform these tasks. Following is bad enough; limping in the rear is far worse. By all the standards that matter in the modern world—economic development and job creation, literacy, educational and scientific achievement, political freedom and respect for human rights—what was once a mighty civilization has indeed fallen low.

> *"The long quest for freedom [in Muslim countries] has left a string of shabby tyrannies, ranging from traditional autocracies to dictatorships."*

The Blame Game

"Who did this to us?" is of course a common human response when things are going badly, and many in the Middle East, past and present, have asked this question. They have found several different answers. It is usually easier and always more satisfying to blame others for one's misfortunes. For a long time the Mongols were the favorite villains. The Mongol invasions of the thirteenth century were blamed for the destruction of both Muslim power and Islamic civilization, and for what was seen as the ensuing weakness and stagnation. But after a while historians, Muslims and others, pointed to two flaws in this argument. The first was that some of the greatest cultural achievements of Islam, notably in Iran, came after, not before, the Mongol invasions. The second, more difficult to accept but nevertheless undeniable, was that the Mongols overthrew an empire that was already fatally weakened; indeed, it is hard to see how the once mighty empire of the caliphs would otherwise have succumbed to a horde of nomadic horsemen riding across the steppes from East Asia.

The rise of nationalism—itself an import from Europe—produced new perceptions. Arabs could lay the blame for their troubles on the Turks, who had ruled them for many centuries. Turks could lay the blame for the stagnation of their civilization on the dead weight of the Arab past, in which the creative energies of the Turkish people were caught and immobilized. Persians could lay the blame for the loss of their ancient glories on Arabs, Turks, and Mongols impartially.

In the nineteenth and twentieth centuries British and French paramountcy in much of the Arab world produced a new and more plausible scapegoat—Western imperialism. In the Middle East there have been good reasons for such blame. Western political domination, economic penetration, and—longest, deepest, and most insidious of all—cultural influence changed the face of the region and transformed the lives of its people, turning them in new directions, arousing new hopes and fears, creating new dangers and new expectations without precedent in their cultural past.

But the Anglo-French interlude was comparatively brief and ended half a century ago; Islam's change for the worse began long before and continued unabated afterward. Inevitably, the role of the British and the French as villains was taken over by the United States, along with other aspects of Western leadership. The attempt to transfer the guilt to America has won considerable support but, for similar reasons, remains unconvincing. Anglo-French rule and American influence, like the Mongol invasions, were a consequence, not a cause, of the inner weakness of Middle Eastern states and societies. Some observers, both inside and outside the region, have pointed to differences in the post-colonial development of former British possessions—for example, between Aden, in the Middle East, and Singapore or Hong Kong; or between the various lands that once made up the British Empire in India.

> *"The relegation of women to an inferior position in Muslim society . . . deprives the Islamic world of the talents and energies of half its people."*

Another European contribution to this debate is anti-Semitism, and blaming "the Jews" for all that goes wrong. Jews in traditional Islamic societies experienced the normal constraints and occasional hazards of minority status. Until the rise and spread of Western tolerance in the seventeenth and eighteenth centuries, they were better off under Muslim than under Christian rule in most significant respects. With rare exceptions, where hostile stereotypes of the Jew existed in the Islamic tradition, Islamic societies tended to be contemptuous and dismissive rather than suspicious and obsessive.

This made the events of 1948—the failure to prevent the establishment of the state of Israel—all the more of a shock. As some writers observed at the time, it was humiliating enough to be defeated by the great imperial powers of the West; to suffer the same fate at the hands of a contemptible gang of Jews was intolerable. Anti-Semitism and its image of the Jew as a scheming, evil monster provided a soothing antidote.

The earliest specifically anti-Semitic statements in the Middle East occurred among Christian minorities and can usually be traced back to European originals. They had limited impact; during the Dreyfus trial in France, for example, when a Jewish officer was unjustly accused and condemned by a hostile court, Muslim comments usually favored the persecuted Jew against his Christian persecutors. But the poison continued to spread, and starting in 1933, Nazi Germany and its various agencies made a concerted and on the whole remarkably successful effort to promote European-style anti-Semitism in the Arab world. The struggle for Palestine greatly facilitated the acceptance of the anti-Semitic interpretation of history, and led some to attribute all evil in the Middle East—and, indeed, in the world—to secret Jewish plots. This interpretation has pervaded much of the public discourse in the region, including that seen in education, the media, and even entertainment.

An argument sometimes adduced is that the cause of the changed relationship between East and West is not a Middle Eastern decline but a Western upsurge—the discoveries and the scientific, technological, industrial, and political revolutions that transformed the West and vastly increased its wealth and power. But this is merely to restate the question: Why did the discoverers of America sail from Spain rather than from a Muslim Atlantic port, out of which such voyages were indeed attempted in earlier times? Why did the great scientific breakthrough occur in Europe and not, as one might reasonably have expected, in the richer, more advanced, and in most respects more enlightened realm of Islam?

Islam and Freedom

A more sophisticated form of the blame game finds its targets inside, rather than outside, Islamic society. One such target is religion—for some, specifically Islam. But to blame Islam as such is usually hazardous and not often attempted. Nor is it very plausible. For most of the Middle Ages it was neither the older cultures of the Orient nor the newer cultures of the West that were the major centers of civilization and progress but the world of Islam. There old sciences were recovered and developed and new sciences were created; there new industries were born and manufactures and commerce were expanded to a level without precedent. There, too, governments and societies achieved a freedom of thought and expression that led persecuted Jews and even dissident Christians to flee Christendom for refuge in Islam. In comparison with modern ideals, and even with modern practice in the more advanced democracies, the medieval Islamic world offered only limited freedom, but that was vastly more than was offered by any of its predecessors, its contemporaries, or most of its successors.

The point has often been made: If Islam is an obstacle to freedom, to science, to economic development, how is it that Muslim society in the past was a pioneer in all three—and this when Muslims were much closer in time to the sources and inspiration of their faith than they are now? Some have posed the question in a different form—not "What has Islam done to the Muslims?" but

"What have the Muslims done to Islam?"—and have answered by laying the blame on specific teachers and doctrines and groups.

For those known nowadays as Islamists or fundamentalists, the failures and shortcomings of modern Islamic lands afflict those lands because they adopted alien notions and practices. They fell away from authentic Islam and thus lost their former greatness. Those known as modernists or reformers take the opposite view, seeing the cause of this loss not in the abandonment but in the retention of old ways, and especially in the inflexibility and ubiquity of the Islamic clergy, who, they say, are responsible for the persistence of beliefs and practices that might have been creative and progressive a thousand years ago but are neither today. The modernists' usual tactic is not to denounce religion as such, still less Islam in particular, but to level their criticism against fanaticism. It is to fanaticism—and more particularly to fanatical religious authorities—that they attribute the stifling of the once great Islamic scientific movement and, more generally, of the freedom of thought and expression.

> *"Lack of freedom . . . underlies so many of the troubles of the Muslim world."*

A more common approach to this theme has been to discuss a specific problem: the place of religion and of its professional exponents in the political order. In this view a principal cause of Western progress is the separation of Church and State and the creation of a civil society governed by secular laws. Another approach has been to view the main culprit as the relegation of women to an inferior position in Muslim society, which deprives the Islamic world of the talents and energies of half its people and entrusts the other half's crucial early years of upbringing to illiterate and downtrodden mothers. The products of such an education, it has been said, are likely to grow up either arrogant or submissive, and unfit for a free, open society. However one evaluates the views of secularists and feminists, their success or failure will be a major factor in shaping the Middle Eastern future.

Some solutions that once commanded passionate support have been discarded. The two dominant movements in the twentieth century were socialism and nationalism. Both have been discredited—the first by its failure, the second by its success and consequent exposure as ineffective. Freedom, interpreted to mean national independence, was seen as the great talisman that would bring all other benefits. The overwhelming majority of Muslims now live in independent states, but this has brought no solutions to their problems. National socialism, the bastard offspring of both ideologies, persists in a few states that have preserved the Nazi-Fascist style of dictatorial government and indoctrination through a vast security apparatus and a single all-powerful part. These regimes have failed every test except survival and have brought none of the promised benefits. If anything, their infrastructures are even more antiquated than those of other Muslim states, their armed forces designed primarily for terror and repression.

At present two answers to the question of what went wrong command widespread support in the Middle East, each with its own diagnosis and corresponding prescription. One attributes all evil to the abandonment of the divine heritage of Islam and advocates return to a real or imagined past. That is the way of the Iranian revolution and of the so-called fundamentalist movements and regimes in various Muslim countries. The other condemns the past and advocates secular democracy, best embodied in the Turkish Republic, proclaimed in 1923 by Kemal Atatürk.

For the oppressive but ineffectual governments that rule much of the Middle East, finding targets to blame serves a useful, indeed an essential, purpose—to explain the poverty that they have failed to alleviate and to justify the tyranny that they have introduced. They seek to deflect the mounting anger of their unhappy subjects toward other, outside targets.

Muslim Civilization at a Crossroad

But growing numbers of Middle Easterners are adopting a more self-critical approach. The question "Who did this to us?" has led only to neurotic fantasies and conspiracy theories. And the question "What did we do wrong?" has led naturally to a second question: "How do we put it right?" In that question, and in the various answers that are being found, lie the best hopes for the future.

The worldwide exposure given to the views and actions of [terrorist] Osama bin Laden and his hosts the Taliban [the oppressive regime in Afghanistan] has provided a new and vivid insight into the eclipse of what was once the greatest, most advanced, and most open civilization in human history.

To a Western observer, schooled in the theory and practice of Western freedom, it is precisely the lack of freedom—freedom of the mind from constraint and indoctrination, to question and inquire and speak; freedom of the economy from corrupt and pervasive mismanagement; freedom of women from male oppression; freedom of citizens from tyranny—that underlies so many of the troubles of the Muslim world. But the road to democracy, as the Western experience amply demonstrates, is long and hard, full of pitfalls and obstacles.

If the peoples of the Middle East continue on their present path, the suicide bomber may become a metaphor for the whole region, and there will be no escape from a downward spiral of hate and spite, rage and self-pity, poverty and oppression, culminating sooner or later in yet another alien domination—perhaps from a new Europe reverting to old ways, perhaps from a resurgent Russia, perhaps from some expanding superpower in the East. But if they can abandon grievance and victimhood, settle their differences, and join their talents, energies, and resources in a common creative endeavor, they can once again make the Middle East, in modern times as it was in antiquity and in the Middle Ages, a major center of civilization. For the time being, the choice is theirs.

International Efforts to Promote Democracy in Developing Nations Are Sometimes Counterproductive

by Eric Bjornlund

About the author: *Eric Bjornlund is a former senior associate of Asia programs at the National Democratic Institute for International Affairs.*

Hardly an election occurs outside the developed world today without an international corps of observers flying in to certify the results. But the outsiders sometimes do more harm than good.

Friends and foes of the United States smirked in fall 2000 as the champion of the free world waded in embarrassment through Florida's electoral swamps. Even as U.S. government agencies and nonprofit groups were busily monitoring "troubled" elections in half a dozen foreign lands, from Haiti to Azerbaijan, America's presidential election was thrown into doubt by arthritic voting technology, sloppy voter registration, and partisan election officials—flaws that were supposed to afflict only "less developed" countries. One Brazilian pundit half-seriously called for international sanctions to force a new vote in Florida.

But American democracy has never been faultless, and—derisive comments in the international press notwithstanding—U.S. efforts to promote democracy abroad have never been predicated on its perfection at home. Indeed, the American groups that work to spread representative government overseas have drawn heavily on non-American models precisely because they recognize the shortcomings and idiosyncrasies of the U.S. system.

The real flaws in the global effort to foster democracy, meanwhile, have gone largely unnoticed—and they are flaws that threaten great harm to the democratic cause. The scattered and diffuse democracy movement of decades past has been transformed into a worldwide industry of sorts, led but not controlled by the United States. The industry has done much good. But it has also put a stamp of legitimacy on Potemkin-village democracies in Cambodia, Egypt, Armenia, and other countries. It has frustrated local democratic activists from Indonesia to Peru, and it has provided autocratic rulers with ammunition to dismiss courageous local democrats as lackeys of foreign powers. Worst of all, it has undermined efforts to apply uniform democratic standards around the world.

The democracy industry has its deepest roots in the United States. From the time of President Woodrow Wilson's crusade to "make the world safe for democracy" to the era of the Cold War, Americans of virtually all political persuasions shared an ideological commitment to advancing the democratic cause in the world. But only under the Reagan administration did the United States begin to focus and institutionalize its efforts. Washington now devotes some $700 million annually to democracy promotion. Much of it is channeled through the Agency for International Development—which parcels out the money to private consulting firms and more than a score of nongovernmental organizations, such as the Carter Center and the Asia Foundation—and a small but significant portion goes to the congressionally-chartered National Endowment for Democracy. It is a substantial commitment, equal to about 10 percent of the entire U.S. foreign aid budget.

The United States, however, is outspent by others. The European Union and developed countries such as Japan and Australia, along with multilateral organizations such as the United Nations, the World Bank, and the Organization for Security and Cooperation in Europe, also pour large amounts of monetary, human, and diplomatic capital into the global crusade. The stated purposes are the same: fighting corruption, establishing the rule of law, fostering civil society, developing democratic parliaments, and monitoring elections. But not all of the industry's "players" share the same commitment to democracy, and some are willing to sacrifice its pursuit to other foreign-policy goals.

The industry's rise has coincided with a revolutionary expansion of democracy around the world. What Harvard University political scientist Samuel Huntington has called the "third wave" of democratization began in the late 1970s with political transitions in Spain and Portugal, and spread in the 1980s to Latin America and Asia. Democracy swept through Eastern and Central Europe after the

> *"The ... flaws in the global effort to foster democracy ... threaten great harm to the democratic cause."*

fall of the Berlin Wall in 1989 and continued after the breakup of the Soviet Union. The 1990s also saw dramatic political openings in Africa and Asia. Since 1988, a total of 50 countries have made the transition to democracy, from Poland and Brazil to Taiwan and Nigeria.

The democracy industry can't claim credit for the third wave, but it has reinforced the trend. Last year, under the weight of domestic and international pressure, repressive regimes in Yugoslavia and Peru fell after election monitors helped expose their attempts to manipulate national elections. Two decades ago, such a feat would have been almost unimaginable.

The industry has been fortunate: Its successes have been more sensational than its failures. But an examination of highly publicized elections, such as the recent ones in Cambodia and Indonesia, shows that its failures can be deleterious.

I worked in both countries as an official of the National Democratic Institute for International Affairs (NDI), one of the four main nongovernmental organizations supported by the National Endowment for Democracy. (Each of the two major political parties sponsors an organization, and organized labor and business sponsor the other two.) While my work involved several areas of democracy promotion, the monitoring of elections best illustrates the tensions caused by the involvement of foreign activists. I have seen outside monitors contribute to public confidence in the integrity of elections, provide invaluable moral support to democratic activists facing authoritarian regimes, and deter fraud. But I have also seen them stumble—and do great harm to many of the world's fragile democracies.

> *"I have ... seen [foreign democracy activists] stumble—and do great harm to many of the world's fragile democracies."*

The Disastrous "Miracle on the Mekong"

Cambodia suffered more violent turmoil than almost any other country in the 20th century. It endured intense American bombing during the last years of the Vietnam War, and three years (1975–78) of terror under the communist Khmer Rouge, which, according to some estimates, left nearly a quarter of the Asian country's 8 million people dead. A Vietnamese invasion in 1978 was followed by more than a decade of civil war.

In 1991, a glimmer of hope appeared when Cambodia signed an internationally sponsored peace agreement calling for liberal democracy and genuine elections. The United Nations established the largest, most costly peacekeeping force in its history (15,000 troops and a budget of $2 billion) to organize the election of a new government and administer the country during its transition. But the 1993 election failed to bring either democracy or stability, and in 1997 First Prime Minister Prince Ranariddh was overthrown in a bloody coup by his putative coalition partner, former communist Hun Sen. The United States and other countries suspended aid, and the United Nations denied the new government a seat in the General Assembly.

Hun Sen eventually agreed to a new election. But the international community was far from united in its approach. Though democracy watchers around the world deplored Hun Sen's violent putsch, many diplomats and aid providers believed that Cambodia could not be governed effectively without him. To them, an election—even an imperfect one—that lent Hun Sen legitimacy but also preserved a niche for political opposition seemed to be the best Cambodia could hope for.

With decisions about the future of foreign aid and diplomatic relations hinging on judgments about whether the contest was "free and fair," the pressure was on to grant it a clean bill of health—giving Hun Sen a sense of how much he could get away with. Eager to end the political crisis, the European Union, the United Nations, Japan, and Australia offered money, equipment, and technical assistance for the administration of Hun Sen's far-from-perfect election.

The Americans were more squeamish about lending legitimacy to a dubious election. But the U.S. government tried to have it both ways: It declined to offer election aid—but watched from a distance, poised to resume aid and improve diplomatic relations if the process miraculously turned out well.

One Cambodian newspaper dubbed the Americans "idealists" and the Europeans "pragmatists." But the difference was rooted in more than attitude. The United States, with its long history of activism by independent human-rights and prodemocracy groups, has largely separated election monitoring from foreign policy. In its efforts to monitor elections abroad, the United States relies heavily on nongovernmental organizations such as NDI and the International Republican Institute (IRI). These groups have a single, clear mission: to further democracy. It's then up to the government to make decisions about whether and how to engage or aid foreign governments. Other players in the democracy industry assign diplomats and bureaucrats to monitor elections. Their judgments are inevitably colored by the fact that democracy is only one of the ends they seek.

Cambodia held its much anticipated [election] on July 26, 1998. Despite the atmosphere of intimidation created by Hun Sen and his followers, an astonishing 97 percent of Cambodian voters turned out to cast their ballots. Domestic monitoring groups described the process as relatively peaceful and well administered, as did the hundreds of assembled international observers. Speaking before a packed press conference at the plush Le Royale Hotel two days after the election, our own delegation's coleader, former representative Steven Solarz (D.-N.Y.), went so far as to speculate that the election might one day be seen as "the miracle on the Mekong."

Hun Sen's Cambodian People's Party (CPP) was declared the winner of approximately 42 percent of the ballots cast, which translated into a 64-seat majority of the 122-member assembly. Prince Ranariddh's constitutional monarchist party won 31 percent of the vote and 43 seats, and a second opposition party, led by activist Sam Rainsy, won 14 percent and 15 seats.

Violence and Corruption Mar the Election

But the Cambodian election was no miracle. Politically motivated killings had been commonplace since the '97 coup, and they stopped only weeks before the election. Opposition members of Parliament, led by Ranariddh and Sam Rainsy, had fled the country in fear of their lives after the coup. Though opposition leaders were induced to return in early 1998, the violence hardly provided the backdrop for a "free and fair" democratic competition.

Violence was not all that marred the election: The CPP government denied opposition parties access to radio and television, threatened opposition supporters, and banned political demonstrations in the capital city of Phnom Penh during the campaign. Hun Sen's supporters freely exploited their control of the judiciary and security forces. Two weeks before election day, an NDI-IRI report concluded that the process up to that point was "fundamentally flawed."

> *"International democracy groups [in Cambodia] erred by making election day the big media event."*

Some foreign observers, however, failed to report these problems or blithely dismissed all signs of trouble. While the United States funded 25 long-term observers recruited through the Asia Foundation, none of their reports were made public or shared with other observer groups. The Joint International Observer Group (JIOG), a UN-organized umbrella organization of 34 delegations with some 500 members, didn't even wait for the initial ballot count or for its own observers to return from the field before it endorsed the process as "free and fair to an extent that enables it to reflect, in a credible way, the will of the Cambodian people."

Among the JIOG's grab bag of groups were delegations dispatched by the governments of Burma, China, and Vietnam—regimes hardly known for their democratic credentials. One JIOG delegation, which openly positioned itself as a Hun Sen apologist, urged even before balloting began that the election "not be discredited for reasons of international politics." Most troubling of all, however, was the tendency of the JIOG's democratic members—the "pragmatic" Europeans and Japanese—to gloss over the election's undemocratic features.

Notwithstanding Solarz's hyperbolic "miracle" remark, the NDI-IRI assessment as a whole was quite levelheaded. It made clear our concern about "violence, extensive intimidation, unfair media access, and ruling party control of the administrative machinery." British politician Glenys Kinnock, speaking for the delegation from the European Union, rendered a terse and similarly restrained verdict—one that implicitly distanced the EU observers from both the "miracle" statement and the JIOG's unqualified endorsement. Indeed, Solarz himself had said that the election would prove a "miracle" only if the tranquility of election day prevailed, and if the subsequent grievance process and the formation of the government proceeded smoothly. But in most press accounts, little more than Solarz's sound bite survived.

The press, however, was not really to blame for the world's failure to come to terms with what happened in Cambodia. As they have in many other cases, international democracy groups erred by making election day the big media event. By bringing observers to Cambodia only days before the polls opened, issuing much anticipated (and hastily composed) assessments of the polling, and hopping on the next plane home, monitoring groups encouraged journalists to zero in on "E-Day"—which constituted, after all, only 24 hours of a months-long process.

It didn't take long for things in Cambodia to fall apart, making the foreign observers' upbeat assessments of the election seem all the more disconnected from reality. ("Sometimes I wonder if we're in the same Cambodia," one exasperated local democrat said.) After struggling to complete the vote count, including a perfunctory attempt to conduct a recount in a few token locations, the CPP-dominated election commission and constitutional court summarily dismissed the numerous complaints filed by opposition parties. After election day, it was revealed that the election commission had secretly altered the formula for allocating seats, thus giving Hun Sen a majority in the National Assembly. There is some evidence that the commission was only responding to international advisers who wanted to correct their own technical mistake. No matter. The change was made in secret, depriving the election of whatever shred of legitimacy it might have claimed.

In Phnom Penh and other Cambodian cities, post-election protests turned violent. One man was killed. The formation of a new government stalled amid finger pointing and threats.

One month after the election, our group decried the violence and utter lack of an appeals process. But our warnings went unheeded. The army of observers and reporters was gone, and international attention had waned. Neither the United Nations, nor the European Union, nor the JIOG ever made a single additional public statement after their relatively positive assessments immediately following election day. That would have required them to confront uncomfortable facts.

Three years after the "miracle on the Mekong," Hun Sen presides over a corrupt and undemocratic regime. His security forces regularly harass opponents and commit rape, extortion, and extra judicial killings with impunity. But, with American support, the Hun Sen regime has regained Cambodia's seat in the United Nations, and the flow of foreign aid, including American aid, has resumed.

The Mishandled Indonesian Presidential Election

A year after the dismal proceedings in Cambodia, Indonesia held a much happier and more legitimate election—its first genuinely democratic contest in 44 years. Many of the democracy-industry circuit riders who had been in Cambodia promptly turned their attention to the archipelago. But again, the global democracy industry made serious mistakes, perhaps missing a once-in-a-generation opportunity to shore up a fragile new democracy.

Indonesia's democratic opening came in May 1998, when public anger at the regime's corruption and economic mismanagement forced an aging President Suharto to step down after 32 years as the country's autocratic leader. Democratic activists in Indonesia quickly organized the most extensive domestic election-monitoring effort ever seen. The prospect of establishing democracy in the country with the world's largest Islamic population helped open foreign wallets. By early 1999, the United Nations Development Program and the interim government in Jakarta had launched an effort to raise $90 million in international contributions for election administration, voter education, and poll watching. Just over a third of the total was to come from the United States.

> *"In their drive to ensure fair procedures, the well-intentioned outsiders inadvertently disrupted the efforts of Indonesia's many democrats."*

When the polls opened on June 7, 1999, more than half a million Indonesians and nearly 600 foreigners from 30 countries were on hand to monitor the proceedings. It can only be called a messy election—but the vote was undeniably democratic. In the subsequent indirect election of the president, moderate Islamic leader Ahdurrahman Wahid pulled out a surprising victory. Unfortunately, he has been ineffective, and the Indonesian national legislature now looks poised to remove him from office. Whether he stays or goes, Indonesia seems bound to endure a period of turmoil.

In Indonesia, the democracy industry inflicted a subtler form of damage than it did in Cambodia. In their drive to ensure fair procedures, the well-intentioned outsiders inadvertently disrupted the efforts of Indonesia's many democrats. They once again allowed too much attention to focus on election day. And they stole the spotlight from local groups that could have benefited from more media attention. The sudden influx of foreign money—much of it dumped into the country only weeks, or even days, before the election—touched off a mad scramble among the Indonesian groups. At the very moment they should have been focusing on the logistics of election monitoring, they were pouring their time and energy into grant proposals and budgets. Huge sums encouraged infighting among the Indonesian organizations. Misguided donors often made things worse by favoring different groups or factions.

Foreign aid also encouraged the needless proliferation of new monitoring groups—organizations with little experience and even less commitment. Twelve months before the election, only one monitoring group existed in Indonesia. The next nine months witnessed the appearance of two more. But in the two months before the election, some 90 more groups elbowed their way to the table. New organizations sprang up like American dot-com companies in the heyday of high-tech opportunism—and many of them showed just as little resiliency.

Having created incentives for Indonesians to compete with one another, the donors then tried to compel them to join forces in ways that didn't always make sense. The monitoring groups, for example, were required to divide their responsibilities along geographical lines, which touched off new struggles as leaders haggled over their territories. The division could more effectively have been made along, say, functional lines, with some groups looking into such matters as pre-election complaints while others educated voters or monitored vote counts. In any event, it was a decision best left to local activists, not outsiders.

As the head of the NDI's 20-person professional team in Indonesia, I saw firsthand some of the ill effects of all this. Three weeks before election day, at a final planning meeting of the University Network for Free Elections held at the University of Indonesia in Jakarta, I was pained to see the group's leaders mired in arguments over money. For three days, student leaders from around the country complained about inadequate budgets, criticized the headquarters for hoarding money, and made apparently specious allegations of corruption. The urgent issues at hand—volunteer training, communications systems, vote count monitoring—went virtually undiscussed.

For the University Network's idealistic national leaders, such as human rights lawyer Todung Mulya Lubis and professor Smita Notosusanto, it was a profoundly dispiriting experience. After the election, they and their colleagues abandoned any ambitions of building a national grassroots prodemocracy network, instead creating a Jakarta-based advocacy organization called the Center for Electoral Reform.

The Indonesian experience is a reminder that elections are not an end in themselves; they are, rather, one step in the ongoing process of building democracy. Local organizations and networks created to monitor elections often go on to promote democracy in other ways, by fighting corruption, monitoring government performance, or engaging in civic education. They must be strengthened, with moral as well as material support, not treated like voting machines or ballot boxes to be stored away until the next election.

> *"With experience, attention, and care, many of the ills that beset the new global democracy industry can be overcome."*

The democracy industry did a few things right in Indonesia. Not least, it helped ensure fair elections. And former president Jimmy Carter, the reigning celebrity in the international observer corps, offered a fine example of how foreign observers should behave. Carter was a careful student of the election, studying verification techniques, visiting polling stations, and listening to the reports of Indonesian monitors. On the day after the polls closed, he was enthusiastic. But hours before he was to address a press conference, he agreed to meet a small group of Indonesian democracy activists. They were worried about more talk of miracles. Carter listened, and he went before the television cameras with a very different message. He expressed optimism, but he also emphasized the need to pay attention in the days ahead as the votes were counted, the president was selected, and the new government took power. Carter focused attention where it belongs: on the long-term process of building democracy and the local groups that make it work.

Reforming the Democracy Industry

With experience, attention, and care, many of the ills that beset the new global democracy industry can be overcome. Shifting attention from election day to the months before and after voters go to the polls is a matter of common sense. Such a shift would also underscore the broader point that genuine democratization takes time, and that those who are sincere in their efforts to help must commit for the long term. Democratization, says Cambodian opposition leader Rainsy, depends on political forces "who'll remain here, who'll fight here, who'll die here, and who are determined to fight for democracy—not just observers who come for a few days." There should be nothing controversial about helping local democratic activists become continuing players with a stake in their country's future. But because so many of the democracy industry's important actors regard representative government as just one goal, to be balanced against others, this will be difficult to achieve.

All elections must be judged honestly, by the same internationally recognized standards. We know what they are: In addition to fair balloting and counting, there must be opportunities for political parties to compete, reasonably equitable access to the news media, an impartial election administration, freedom from political intimidation, and prompt and just resolution of election-related grievances. But until international donors break the link between the promotion of democracy and other foreign-policy goals—something only the United States has attempted—diplomatic goals will inevitably dilute efforts to establish true democratic governance around the world.

The United States is often criticized for taking a retrograde stance on the environment, national missile defense, and other issues. But when it comes to promoting democracy, Americans are criticized for their crusading idealism. What the Cambodian and Indonesian elections show is that a little more idealism might not be so bad. American nongovernmental groups are motivated by an altruistic desire to help people establish democracy. Whatever the flaws of American assistance, the separation of activities such as election monitoring from the official role of government yields a special kind of commitment. Other countries would do well to emulate the U.S. approach.

In the last decades of the 20th century, democracy established itself as the world's dominant political ideal. Yet much of the world's population has yet to enjoy democratic rights, and the commitment of many ostensibly democratic countries remains questionable. If we are to deliver on the promise of global democracy, those who carry its banner must not compromise its simple principles.

Organizations to Contact

The editors have compiled the following list of organizations concerned with the issues debated in this book. The descriptions are derived from materials provided by the organizations. All have publications or information available for interested readers. The list was compiled on the date of publication of the present volume; the information provided here may change. Be aware that many organizations take several weeks or longer to respond to inquiries, so allow as much time as possible.

Association for Women in Development (AWID)
666 11th St. NW, Suite 450, Washington, DC 20001
(202) 628-0440
website: www.awid.org

AWID is an international membership organization committed to gender equality and a just and sustainable development process. AWID facilitates a three-way exchange among scholars, practitioners, and policymakers in order to develop effective and transformative approaches for improving the lives of women and girls worldwide. AWID publishes *AWIDNews*, a quarterly newsletter that keeps members in touch with changes at AWID and in the global women's movement. It includes reports on recent events, thought pieces on critical issues, upcoming events, and advocacy updates.

Association of Third World Studies (ATWS)
Center for International Studies
PO Box 8106, Georgia Southern University, Statesboro, GA 30460
(912) 681-0548
website: http://itc.gsw.edu/atws

ATWS is the largest professional organization of its kind in the world. With a global membership and chapters in South Asia and Africa, members include academics, practitioners in the area of Third World development, employees of government agencies, and diplomats. The association holds international conferences and publishes *The Journal of Third World Studies, ATWS Conference Proceedings, ATWS Newsletter*, and the *ATWS Area Interest List*.

CARE
151 Ellis St. NE, Atlanta, GA 30303-2439
(800) 521-2273, ext. 999
website: www.care.org

CARE is one of the world's largest international relief and development organizations. CARE helped train the first Peace Corps volunteers in Latin America and became a leader in self-help development and food aid. CARE reaches more than 35 million people in more than 60 developing nations in Africa, Asia, Latin America, and Europe. CARE works to provide basic education for children, economic and social empowerment for women, a stable supply of food and clean water, basic health care, universal immunization of children, and access to family planning services. CARE publishes an annual report and special reports on topics such as Afghanistan, AIDS, and India.

Harvard Institute for International Development (HIID)
14 Story St., Cambridge, MA 02138
(617) 495-2161
website: www.hiid.harvard.edu

HIID brings together the diverse resources of Harvard University to assist developing and transitional nations in crafting policies to accelerate their economic growth and improve the welfare of their people. HIID publishes a series of Development Discussion Papers, as well as papers and policy briefs on its program on Equity And Growth through Economic Research (EAGER).

International Monetary Fund (IMF)
700 19th St. NW, Washington, DC 20431
(202) 623-7430
website: www.imf.org

IMF's purpose is to promote international economic cooperation, to help keep a balance of trade among nations so all benefit from the expansion of trade, and to lend its member nations money when necessary. It acts as a depository of information and statistical data regarding the economic affairs of its members. The fund publishes pamphlets, brochures, fact sheets, the semi-monthly *IMF Survey*, and an annual report.

North American Congress on Latin America (NACLA)
475 Riverside Dr., Suite 454, New York, NY 10115
(212) 870-3146
website: www.nacla.org

NACLA is an independent, nonprofit organization that provides policymakers, analysts, academics, organizers, journalists, and religious and community groups with information on major trends in Latin America and its relations with the United States. The core of NACLA's work is its bimonthly magazine *NACLA Report on the Americas*, the most widely read English language publication in Latin America.

North-South Institute (NSI)
55 Murray St., Suite 200, Ottawa, ON, K1N 5M3 Canada
(613) 241-3535
website: www.nsi-ins.ca

NSI is the only independent, nongovernmental research institute in Canada focused on international development. The institute's research supports global efforts to strengthen international development cooperation, improve governance in developing countries, enhance gender and social responsibility in globalizing markets, and prevent ethnic and other conflict. Its publications include books such as *Journeys Just Begun: From Debt Relief to Poverty Reduction*, briefing papers, special reports, speeches, and an annual report.

Population Council
1 Dag Hammarskjold Plaza, Floor 9, New York, NY 10017-2220
(212) 339-0500
website: www.popcouncil.org

The Population Council is an international, nonprofit institution that conducts research on biomedical, social science, and public health. Focusing on developing countries, the Population Council works to improve family planning and reproductive health services and study the causes and consequences of population growth. The Population Council publishes the *Policy Research Division (PRD) Working Papers* and the periodicals *Population and Development Review* and *Studies in Family Planning*.

United Nations Development Programme (UNDP)
1 United Nations Plaza, New York, NY 10017
(212) 906-5558
website: www.undp.org

The United Nations was established in 1945 to, among other things, help nations cooperate in solving international economic, social, cultural, and humanitarian problems. The UNDP engages in global advocacy and analysis to generate knowledge about and develop policies to aid developing nations. UNDP's primary areas of interest are democratic governance, poverty reduction, environment and sustainable energy, gender, HIV/AIDS, information and communication technology, and crisis prevention and recovery. Numerous reports and facts sheets on these topics are available on the UNDP website.

U.S. Agency for International Development (USAID)
Ronald Reagan Building, Washington, DC 20523-0016
(202) 712-4810
website: www.usaid.gov

USAID is the U.S. government agency that implements America's foreign economic and humanitarian assistance programs and provides assistance to countries recovering from disaster, trying to escape poverty, and engaging in democratic reforms. USAID is an independent federal government agency that receives overall foreign policy guidance from the secretary of state. The public may look up and order USAID documents, reports, and publications by using the agency's online database of 100,000 USAID technical and program documents.

World Bank
1818 H St. NW, Washington, DC 20433
(202) 477-1234
website: www.worldbank.org

The World Bank is the world's largest source of development assistance, providing more than $17 billion in loans to its client countries in 2001. The bank uses its financial resources and its extensive knowledge base to help each developing country onto a path of stable, sustainable, and equitable growth. The bank publishes many books and reports on the economies of the developing world, including *An International Assessment of Healthcare Financing: Lessons for Developing Countries* and *A Chance to Learn: Knowledge and Finance for Education in Sub-Saharan Africa*.

Bibliography

Books

Nancy Birdsall, Allan C. Kelley, and Steven Sinding, eds.
Population Matters: Demographic Change, Economic Growth, and Poverty in the Developing World. New York: Oxford University Press, 2001.

Peter Calvert and Susan Calvert
Politics and Society in the Third World. New York: Longman, 2001.

Thomas Carothers
Aiding Democracy Abroad: The Learning Curve. Washington, DC: Carnegie Endowment for International Peace, 1999.

Catharin E. Dalpino
Deferring Democracy; Promoting Openness in Authoritarian Regimes. Washington, DC: Brookings Institution, 2000.

Martin Dent and Bill Peters
The Crisis of Poverty and Debt in the Third World. Brookfield, VT: Ashgate, 1999.

Elizabeth Economy and Michel Oksenberg, eds.
China Joins the World: Progress and Prospects. New York: Council on Foreign Relations Press, 1999.

Thomas L. Friedman
The Lexus and the Olive Tree: Understanding Globalization. New York: Farrar, Straus, Giroux, 2000.

Anthony Giddens
Runaway World: How Globalization Is Reshaping Our Lives. New York: Routledge, 2000.

Robert N. Gwynne and Cristobal Kay, eds.
Latin America Transformed: Globalization and Modernity. New York: Oxford University Press, 1999.

Lawrence E. Harrison and Samuel P. Huntington, eds.
Culture Matters: How Values Shape Human Progress. New York: Basic Books, 2000.

Jeffrey Haynes
Democracy and Civil Society in the Third World: Politics and New Political Movements. Malden, MA: Polity Press, 1998.

Ray Kiely and Phil Marfleet, eds.
Globalisation and the Third World. London: Routledge, 1998.

David S. Landes
The Wealth and Poverty of Nations: Why Some Are So Rich and Some So Poor. New York: W.W. Norton, 1999.

185

Nicholas R. Lardy *China's Unfinished Economic Revolution.* Washington, DC: Brookings Institution, 1998.

Kuan Yew Lee et al. *From Third World to First: The Singapore Story: 1965–2000.* New York: HarperCollins, 2000.

Bernard Lewis *What Went Wrong?: Western Impact and Middle Eastern Response.* New York: Oxford University Press, 2002.

Michael Maren *The Road to Hell: The Ravaging Effects of Foreign Aid and International Charity.* New York: Free Press, 1997.

George McGovern *The Third Freedom: Ending Hunger in Our Time.* New York: Simon and Schuster, 2001.

William H. Meyer *Human Rights and International Political Economy in Third World Nations.* Westport, CT: Praeger, 1998.

Andrew J. Nathan *China's Transition.* New York: Columbia University Press, 1999.

Marina Ottaway and Thomas Carothers, eds. *Funding Virtue: Civil Society Aid and Democracy Promotion.* Washington, DC: Carnegie Endowment for International Peace, 2000.

Joan Powell, ed. *Alternatives to the Peace Corps: A Directory of Third World and U.S. Volunteer Opportunities (9th Ed.).* Oakland, CA: Food First Books, 2000.

Dani Rodrik *Has Globalization Gone Too Far?* Washington, DC: Institute for International Economics, 1997.

Michael G. Roskin *Hard Road to Democracy: Four Developing Nations.* Upper Saddle River, NJ: Prentice-Hall, 2001.

Robert I. Rotberg *Ending Autocracy, Enabling Democracy: The Tribulations of Africa.* Washington, DC: Brookings Institution, 2002.

World Bank *World Development Report 2000/2001: Attacking Poverty.* New York: Oxford University Press, 2000.

Periodicals

Lisa Anderson "Aran Democracy: Dismal Prospects," *World Policy Journal,* Fall 2001.

Salih Booker and William Minter "Global Apartheid," *Nation,* July 9, 2001.

Rebecca Clay "Renewable Energy: Empowering the Developing World," *Environmental Health Perspectives,* January 2002.

Helena Cobban "Boost U.S. Foreign Aid, Big-Time," *Christian Science Monitor,* December 13, 2001.

Catharin Dalpino "Promoting Democracy *and* Human Rights," *Brookings Review,* Fall 2000.

William Easterly "The Failure of Economic Development," *Challenge,* January/February 2002.

Bibliography

Economist	"Arabs Tiptoe to Democracy," August 7, 1999.
Economist	"No Title; Why the Poor Need Property Rights," March 31, 2001.
Michael Elliott	"Free Trade Hypocrites," *Time,* November 26, 2001.
Jeff Faux	"The Global Alternative," *American Prospect,* July 2, 2001.
Jeff Gates	"With Globalization, Poverty Is Optional," *Humanist,* September 2001.
August Gribbin	"Overpopulated Megacities Face Frightening Future," *Insight on the News,* August 21, 2000.
Paul Johnson	"Under Foreign Flags: The Glories and Agonies of Colonialism," *National Review,* February 11, 2002.
Robert D. Kaplan	"Was Democracy Just a Moment?" *Atlantic,* December 1997.
Mario Vargas Llosa	"The Culture of Liberty," *Foreign Policy,* January 2001.
Luis F. Lopez-Calva	"Child Labor: Myths, Theories and Facts," *Journal of International Affairs,* Fall 2001.
Per Pinstrup-Andersen	"Feeding the World in the New Millennium: Issues for the New U.S. Administration," *Environment,* July 2001.
Rick Rowden	"A World of Debt," *American Prospect,* July 2, 2001.
Jeffrey Sachs	"What's Good for the Poor Is Good for America," *Economist,* July 14, 2001.
Bruce R. Scott	"The Great Divide in the Global Village," *Foreign Affairs,* January/February 2001.
Jeff M. Sellers	"How to Spell Debt Relief," *Christianity Today,* May 21, 2001.
Amartya Sen	"How to Judge Globalism," *American Prospect,* January 1, 2002.
Christian E. Weller and Adam Hersh	"Free Markets and Poverty," *American Prospect,* January 1, 2002.
David W. Yang	"More Aid, More Democracy," *Christian Science Monitor,* March 21, 2002.

Index

Index

Samet, Andrew, 40
Santiago, Chile
  health effects of air pollution in, 42
  pollution control projects in, 46
Sauvy, Alfred, 10
school lunch program
  worldwide, is needed to reduce hunger and
    promote education, 25–27
Schumpeter, Joseph, 142
Second World nations, 10
service industries
  child labor in, 37–38
Sharawi, Huda, 148
Shell, Ellen Ruppel, 28
Shintani, Terry, 33
Silva, Susana Galdos, 105
Simon, Julian, 131, 132
Solarz, Steven, 176
Sosa, Lionel, 160–61, 164
South Africa, 51, 52
Srinivasan, T.N., 75
Stages of Economic Growth, The (Rostow), 155
Stiglitz, Joseph, 113
surveys
  on support for family planning services, 109

"Ten Commandments of Development," 164
Thailand, 51–52
Third World nations
  first use of term, 10
  see also developing nations
"thrifty genotype," 32
Tierney, John J., Jr., 35
Tocqueville, Alexis de, 159, 163–64
Todaro, Michael P., 11, 12
trade
  effects on growth, 74–75
  liberalization of, institutional reforms and,
    57–58
  see also globalization
transnational corporations (TNCs), 55
  cultural imperialism and, 66, 67, 70–72
tuberculosis
  costs of, 51
  cost vs. economic return from treatment
    programs, 52
  deaths from, 50
Tynes, J. Scott, 65

United Nations
  Conference on Trade and Development, 117
  Food and Agricultural Organization, 14
  International Conference on Population and
    Development (Cairo, 1994), 125
United Nations Fund for Population Activities,
  128
United Nations International Children's Fund
  (UNICEF), 12
United Nations Population Fund (UNFPA), 102
  cutback in U.S. funding for, 107
United States
  foreign aid spending of, 85

benefits of, 91–92
should increase aid to developing nations,
  86–89
  con, 110–16
should promote democracy in developing
  nations, 150–53
  con, 173–81
should support family planning services,
  102–109
  con, 124–32
United States Agency for International
  Development (USAID), 103–104, 114, 126, 150
  on costs of reducing hunger, 24
  cut in funding of family planning services of,
    108
  objectives of, for promotion of democracy, 151
    civil society, 153
    elections/political processes, 152–53
    governance, 153
    rule of law, 151–52

Vargas Llosa, Álvaro, 160
Vargas Llosa, Mario, 159
Véliz, Claudio, 159

wars
  as cause of world hunger, 25
  twentieth-century, deaths from, 22
Wealth and Poverty of Nations, The (Landes), 166
Weber, Max, 155, 163
Wheeler, David, 41
White, Harry Dexter, 112, 113
Wilson, Woodrow, 174
women
  deaths of, from childbirth and pregnancy, 105
  educational opportunities for, 17
  education for, and link with family size, 26
  illiteracy among, 156
  reproductive control is not in best interests of,
    125–26
  rights of, in Middle East, 148
Women's Environment and Development
  Organization, 125
World Bank, 15, 96
  on costs of malnutrition, 24
  establishment of, 113
  function of, 85
  requirements of, for debt relief, 121
World Development Report 1980, 19
World Development Report 1990, 19
World Health Organization (WHO), 105
World Press Freedom Committee (WPFC), 68
World Trade Organization (WTO), 56
  reforms required by, 59, 60
Worldwatch Institute, 33

Yang, David W., 134
Yeltsin, Boris, 143

Zakaria, Fareed, 143
Zimbabwe, 142
Zimmet, Paul, 31